This book is for all those who struggle with the insidious killer disease called workaholism. It is for those who know that facing the reality of work addiction is to meet the wrath of society. It is for all who long for life-giving workplaces and a saner society.

Working Ourselves to Death

The High Cost of Workaholism,
The Rewards of Recovery

Diane Fassel

HarperSanFrancisco
A Division of HarperCollins*Publishers*

WORKING OURSELVES TO DEATH. Copyright © 1990 by Diane Fassel. All rights reserved. Printed in the United States of America. No part of this book may be used or reproduced in any manner whatsoever without written permission except in the case of brief quotations embodied in critical articles and reviews. For information address HarperCollins Publishers, 10 East 53rd Street, New York, NY 10022.

FIRST EDITION

Library of Congress Cataloging in Publication Data

Fassel, Diane.
    Working ourselves to death : the high cost of workaholism, and the rewards of recovery / Diane Fassel.—1st ed.
      p.   cm.
    Includes index.
    ISBN 0–06–254869–7
    1. Job stress.   2. Workaholics—Psychology.   3. Workaholics—United States.   I. Title.
    HF5548.85.F37   1990
    362.2—dc20   90-38586
                                                               CIP

90 91 92 93 94 HAD 10 9 8 7 6 5 4 3 2 1

This edition is printed on acid-free paper that meets the American National Standards Institute Z39.48 Standard.

Contents

Preface:
A Resounding Silence

Sometimes, in the course of our research, we stumble on a detail that appears interesting but insignificant. Later that detail unravels an entire world of information, in fact becomes a body of knowledge itself. This is exactly what happened to me several years ago.

Anne Wilson Schaef and I were writing a book called *The Addictive Organization,* about the ways organizations operate like active addicts in our society. As we developed the book, it was apparent to us that workaholism was the "cleanest" of all the addictions and the one most prized by corporations. What organization wouldn't want a workaholic employee instead of a drunk falling down on the job?

To better understand work addiction, we did a computerized library search of everything that had been written on the topic in the last ten years. We were amazed to discover that almost nothing had been written on work addiction, although countless articles were available on stress and burnout. I was incredulous that a term that fell smoothly from most people's lips had received scant attention from researchers, health practitioners, and addiction treatment professionals. Indeed, there seemed a deliberate denial of work addiction by both the affected and the afflicted.

Schaef and I noted these things in our book, wrote several papers on the role of work addiction in the addictive organization, and moved on to other aspects of our topic.

One year later, as we promoted *The Addictive Organization* on radio and television, almost every interviewer wanted to discuss workaholism, one of the smallest issues raised in our book. On call-in radio shows, men and women identified themselves as work addicted or struggling at home or in the company with such addicts. On lecture tours, we would casually, almost rhetorically, ask: "Who's a workaholic here?" A sea of hands would wave, and afterward we would be approached by scores of people asking how they could find help for their problem. Obviously, something was happening here.

Within the year that we promoted *The Addictive Organization*, over 150 articles appeared on work addiction. The first Workaholics Anonymous groups have begun, and some forward-looking organizations are recognizing that work addiction is on a par with alcohol addiction.

We have much to uncover and learn about this progressive, fatal disease, which masquerades as a positive trait in the cultural lore of our nation. For, truly, work addiction is one of the most difficult addictions to face. This is due, in part, to the active support it receives from such powerful institutions as the church, the school, and the corporation. Today, there is the same level of awareness regarding workaholism as there was about alcoholism fifty years ago. Even those few authors writing on this topic contribute to the confusion and denial by identifying Type A personalities and workaholics as difficult to live around, but not dangerous to themselves or others.

I do not share the perception of these writers. In the two years I have been observing, researching, and interviewing, I have encountered so many people who are literally dying of their workaholism that I cannot take this disease lightly. We have here a killer. It is more widespread than we had imagined. Surely our denial of workaholism supports some societal processes we are unwilling to confront.

I wrote this book to describe the characteristics of the disease of workaholism in the individual, the family, and the organization, for noticing and naming are themselves liberating. But this is not enough. At a deeper level, I believe we must look into the fabric of a society that careens dangerously close to annihilation because of its refusal to acknowledge its complicity with and dependence on the addictive process in all its manifestations.

Finally, a note about terminology. Bryan E. Robinson, in his book *Work Addiction: Hidden Legacies of Adult Children*, chooses to use "work addict" instead of "workaholic." He does so because the term *workaholic* has had positive connotations attached to it in earlier books and articles.[1] I think there is merit in his choice, in that "work addict" is a stark naming of the actual reality. Also, it reflects a key insight of Twelve-Step recovery groups: "You have a disease, you are not your disease."

As for the term *workaholic*, Wayne Otis first coined it in 1968, although the addiction to work had been around as long as the other addictions and predates 1968. Additionally, the recently formed Workaholics Anonymous groups use the latter term, and many recovering people refer to themselves as workaholics. Consequently, I choose to use both work addict and workaholic interchangeably. Our awareness of this addictive disease is so new, the field for treatment and recovery so unformed, that I believe we can use both terms, giving them nuances as we go along and remaining open to new learning.

Regardless of what we call it, workaholism is damaging individuals, their relationships, and their workplaces. How this is happening and why is the point of this book.

Acknowledgments

I am indebted to many people who contributed significantly to the process of this book. Susan August and Pat Fabiano made substantial input to my original outline. The training groups in the United States and Europe shared their personal stories of work addiction and responded to my ideas. Gwen DeCino ably typed successive drafts. Linda Lewis, Mary Ann Wells, and Linda Crowder did research and provided professional office backup.

Jonathon Lazear, my agent, and Jan Johnson, my editor, showed again how powerful are the combined forces of warmth, humor, and competence. The staff of the Hotel Astoria in Seefeld, Austria; Captain Masse and the crew of the *Cast Muskox* freighter; and the monks of St. Benedict's Monastery in Snowmass, Colorado, all provided nonworkaholic settings conducive to writing.

I am indebted to Anne Wilson Schaef on at least two scores. She contributed greatly to the development of the idea for this book. More importantly, along with others writing about addictions, I owe her an enormous debt of gratitude for her groundbreaking work in showing that addiction is not just a disease affecting individuals and families but is a process in the entire society. Her writing in this area has added richly to my perspective on work addiction as an organizational and societal disease.

In this age when women are advised to find mentors, I have had the extraordinary luck to have been intimately associated with two women I consider true intellectual, moral, and spiritual giants. I thank Mary Luke Tobin and Helen Sanders for the examples of their lives and for their unflagging support of me and my work.

Finally, to my Boulder family, especially Anne and John and all who have urged me forward in this project, I am truly grateful.

All stories and examples in this book are true; however, specific details have been altered to protect the identities of the people involved.

Introduction: A Killer Disease

I am doing organizational consulting in one of the loveliest areas of the United States, Santa Fe, New Mexico, on a day in which the sky is crystalline, the air is perfect, neither too hot nor too cold, and the client is exciting.

Although organizational consulting is sometimes pure drudgery, this day it is the perfect occupation for me, providing the lucky combination of travel, climate, and challenge. This is my first meeting with the client and, as always, I feel the anticipation of learning why I am really here — consulting being a profession in which the reason you are hired often has little to do with what you actually end up doing!

I am particularly interested in the owner/president of the company. She is a strikingly handsome woman, almost six feet tall with platinum hair. When she enters the room she commands attention. She is clearly the leader and the inspiration behind this fledgling company, which has been wildly successful in developing and marketing high-tech telecommunications devices for home and small businesses.

Five of us sit down around a conference table — the owner, three vice presidents, and me. As we begin the meeting, it appears that the owner is filled with feelings. Even as we go around the table introducing ourselves and saying something about what we do, she is teary. Finally, she interrupts our process. "I have something I need to share with my team," she says.

"Diane, you are the only one who isn't in on this," she continues, "but I have been having tests at the hospital to find out why I am having numbness and blackouts and memory loss. I've just received the results of the tests before this meeting. They find that the nerves and connective tissue in my neck are frayed, and that the condition is irreversible."

The others gasp and murmur.

"What causes this?" I ask.

She shakes her head. "The doctors say it's excessive stress. For eight years I have been working ninety hours a week to get this company up and running. I love it. We've been successful, and now I'm paying the price."

"But you have to stop," I protest. "You are killing yourself."

"I know I am," she says, "but I can't stop, I just can't stop."

Suddenly, Santa Fe feels less than idyllic to me. I realize I am again in the presence of workaholism, a disease that I have been encountering with increasing regularity in my consulting practice. I hear variations on this woman's story in corporations, universities, churches, volunteer clubs, and in families. Everywhere I go it seems people are killing themselves with work, busyness, rushing, caring, and rescuing. Work addiction is a modern epidemic and it is sweeping our land.

Workaholism is a killer stalking our society. John O. Neikirk calls it "the pain others applaud."[1] Bryan Robinson calls it "the only lifeboat guaranteed to sink."[2] I call it the cleanest of all the addictions. It is socially promoted because it is seemingly socially productive.

Whatever one calls it, the fact is that workaholism is a progressive, fatal disease in which a person is addicted to the process of working. As a result of the addiction, the person's life becomes increasingly unmanageable in relation to work, and all other areas of life are affected.

Workaholics exhibit the same characteristics of addiction that one finds in the alcoholic or drug addict or relationship addict or compulsive debtor. Whether the addiction is to a substance or a process, the internal design of the disease is the same. And workaholics share these characteristics. For example, alcoholics will deny the effects of drinking on their lives and on their families. Workaholics will develop an elaborate rationalization for why they must work so hard. An overeater will lie about how much she or he consumes. A workaholic will conveniently "forget" that he detoured to his office while running a household errand. Like other addicts, workaholics are in denial. They are dishonest, controlling, judgmental, perfectionistic, self-centered, dualistic in their thinking, confused, crisis oriented, and ultimately spiritually bankrupt. All of these characteristics keep a person in the addictive process of the disease.

There is some speculation that workaholics may also be addicted to the adrenaline high they experience as a result of pushing themselves so hard. If this were true, workaholism would be a unique addiction, in that it has both a substance component (addiction to adrenaline) and a process component (addiction to the actual process of working). The adrenaline rush and subsequent addiction is particularly dangerous for workaholics: It gives them an inflated estimate of their ability to keep working to the detriment of their bodies, which may be giving out.

The effect of workaholism is a growing compulsiveness about work. The obsession grows completely out of bounds and, in the process, the workaholic is taken out of the present. Essentially, workaholics are no longer "showing up" for life. They are alienated from their own bodies, from their own feelings, from their creativity, and from family and friends. They have been taken over by the compulsion to work and are slaves to it. They no longer own their lives. They are truly the walking dead.

Lest we believe that a job is the sole focus of the workaholic, we should remember that workaholics can also be unemployed, underemployed, or retired. "Work addict" is a broad term that covers rushaholics, careaholics, busyaholics — any person who is driven to do too much, whether that person works sixty hours a week or runs around like a chicken with its head cut off. In its narrowest sense, workaholism is an addiction to action; but the action takes many forms. As we will see later, some work addicts appear motionless, but their minds are racing. The type of action may vary, but the process is the same: You leave yourself.

"Yikes!" you may say. "I love my work — is this me? I sometimes stay long hours, I lose myself in projects. I take work on vacations." This and similar questions have been posed to me on radio shows. "I love my work. Does that make me a workaholic?" (It is interesting that our awareness of this disease is so low that we don't know when we are one! How many heroin addicts, with a needle sticking in their veins, ask such a question?)

Indeed, there are people who love their work and work hard, and there is a world of difference between them and the workaholic. There are times when the healthy worker stays overtime or gets caught up in a project. However, when the task is done, this person is not overcome with depression and panic. The healthy worker gives time and attention to personal relationships. The healthy worker feels tired and honors weariness with rest and time off. Such a person balances his or her life. For the healthy worker, work is only one component of life and it enhances life; for the workaholic, life is diminished. The workaholic cannot say "no" to work and its demands. Rather, the workaholic seeks work because it is the fix, the supply. Whenever workaholics are out of touch with their supply, they feel desperate.

Workaholism is a compulsion, a disease. No amount of willpower will prevent the alcoholic from reaching for a drink; no amount of good resolutions will stop the workaholic. Of course, what compounds the problem for the workaholic is a social structure that rewards work addiction. No wonder my radio call-ins are confused. They have internal signals telling them that something is wrong with the way they are working, but externally our society is giving them a series of positive myths about workaholism. It is through these myths that society establishes work addiction as the norm and numbs us to the disastrous effects of this disease.

1. Workaholism: Reality & Myths

Joe is in his early forties. He has a degree in engineering. He makes $150,000 a year. He drives a sports car, while a station wagon sits in the garage for his wife and for family outings. He lives in a custom home in the suburbs. Joe works an average of sixty hours a week, including weekends. His children are young, and he rarely sees them because he leaves home before they are up and he returns home after they are in bed. Joe has gone months without spending time with his children. He has a medicine cabinet filled with prescription and nonprescription drugs for helping him sleep and for soothing his stomach, which acts up a lot lately. He is never far from his cellular phone or his voice mail. Joe is getting ahead and he says he is happy. This is a myth and Joe is living out of it.

A myth is a powerful belief that often goes unquestioned by the majority of the society. Myths are internalized and become part of the way things are. Often their very power comes from our unquestioning attitude toward them. In the course of my interviews and research for this book, I encountered many myths about workaholism. I think it is important that we see these beliefs for exactly what they are—rationalizations that keep us stuck in the addictive process and in denial about workaholism in particular. Some commonly held myths about workaholism include the following:

- Workaholics are always working.
- Workaholism only affects high-powered executives and Yuppies.

- It's only stress and burnout.
- Workaholism can be "managed" with stress-reduction techniques.
- No one ever died of hard work.
- Workaholism is profitable for corporations.
- Workaholism is a positive addiction.
- Workaholics are super-productive, they get ahead.
- Workaholism only adversely affects the workaholic.
- Workaholics are happy.

Let's take a closer look at the reality behind these mistaken beliefs.

Workaholics Are Always Working

It is true that work addicts work a lot, but it is a myth that they are always working. For some workaholics, the problem is that they are always avoiding work. Thus it would be a mistake to decide that a person who is inactive is not obsessed by work. He or she may be a work anorexic, whose life is as much out of control as the person who overworks.

Some workaholics go on binges — they work in spurts and then take weeks off. The *way* they approach the work is the issue, not the constancy of work.

In the later stages of the disease of workaholism, some work addicts sit and stare into space in a comatose fashion.

Several workaholics I know discussed this myth with me and laughed at the prospect of "always working." "My disease is much trickier than that," said Jake. "If I were always working, my family and friends would be on to me. I'm in front of the TV thinking about work. I'm at the symphony mentally planning work. I'm lying in bed discussing a project with my boss in my head. It's easier that way. No one can accuse me of overworking, and I get to keep my secret and protect my supply." So Jake *is* always working; he just doesn't appear to be to others.

Nor do workaholics need to be doing work all the time. There are unemployed workaholics, housewife workaholics, and workaholics on vacation. It is an issue of identity. A friend who is in a program of recovery from her work addiction observed that she does not feel compulsive about accomplishing tasks all the time. Instead she believes that her identity comes from work. She works well and sanely and she still looks primarily to her doing and her accomplishments to see who she is. I am reminded of the mayor of Indianapolis, who remarked in a television interview, "I went from a human being to a human doing." When work is the sole reservoir for your identity, you are addicted. Work has you, you don't have it.

Workaholism Only Affects High-powered Executives and Yuppies

The media contribute to our myth about high-powered executives, for these are the people who are frequently put before us, boasting about their workaholic lifestyle. Somehow, the myth goes, workaholism comes with the corner office, the power lunches, and the car phone.

On the contrary, workaholism is not particular about its victims. Housewives are frequently work addicted. Several housewife workaholics tell me that they are constantly on the go, routinely putting in sixteen-hour days, all in the interest of being perfect wives and mothers.

There is increasing concern in the United States, Europe, and Japan about the pressures children feel to excel and get ahead, from preschool on. For some of these children, work addiction in the form of excellence in school, extracurricular activities, and sports may be a release from otherwise dysfunctional families; but many are already showing the signs of becoming Type A personalities.

Finally, our social stratification fosters work addiction. There are scores of single parents who are hourly workers who hold two or three jobs because to do otherwise would leave them in abject poverty. For them the compulsion to work may be nil, but the societal pressure to survive is the driving force.

It's Only Stress and Burnout

Inevitably, if workaholism is not interrupted, people burn out; but stress and burnout are not identical with workaholism. Some people may encounter a series of life events that result in physical and emotional exhaustion. They then pull back, take time to heal, perhaps change jobs, and then reenter their lives and work. They learn from such an experience to see the warning signs, and they alter their expectations of themselves and others accordingly.

Workaholics do exhibit stress and burnout, yet their disease is more than stress and burnout. Their disease is chronic and progressive, not acute. It is an entire orientation toward life. To deny the disease concept means that workaholics will use half-measures (like stress-reduction techniques) to treat a disease that affects them physically, emotionally, mentally, and spiritually. "Half-measures availed us nothing," states the Big Book of Alcoholics Anonymous. Addressing only the stress and burnout alleviates the symptoms, but doesn't affect the underlying disease process.

Workaholism Can Be "Managed" with Stress-Reduction Techniques

Not true! Stress can be managed with stress-reduction techniques, but workaholism cannot. In writing *The Addictive Organization*, we were surprised to discover that workaholics are among the healthiest-looking people we had ever seen. Some routinely ate healthful meals and exercised regularly. We subsequently discovered that the devotion to physical health was in the service of protecting their supply. For how can workaholics have contact with their addictive substance (work) if their bodies give out? The stress-reduction techniques actually produce the opposite effect. They enable the workaholic to go on a little longer before experiencing the fatal effects of the disease.

No One Ever Died of Hard Work

I am in Iowa, at a convention of Protestant ministers from around the state. They are ruddy, hardy, hard-working people, mostly ministering in rural communities. The ministers come from farm families, where the motto is, "No one ever died of hard work." They believe this statement, for their experience is that hard work keeps you out of trouble and makes a positive contribution to family and community. Unfortunately, something new is happening in rural Iowa. Young and middle-aged ministers are leaving the ministry—disillusioned and unhappy. Working harder doesn't seem to help. They are burned out on caring.

Hard manual labor may lower your cholesterol count, but workaholism will kill you. It may kill you sooner than other addictions, because the physical effects of the disease are harder to detect due to the workaholic's tendency to regulate diet and exercise. Many workaholics die from heart attacks or become debilitated by strokes. Others place their lives and the lives of others in danger due to blackouts they experience while driving. Having a fatal disease means you die from it eventually. Consequently, every nonrecovering workaholic can say, "I died of the process of work."

Workaholism Is Profitable for Corporations

Guess again! The opposite is true. I hear this myth everywhere I go, and as an organizational consultant I spend a lot of time in corporations. A common complaint of employees and middle managers is that companies foster workaholism. They actively seek and reward the workaholic.

My research has found that workaholics not only do not benefit corporations, they actually end up costing companies money. Some work addicts are erratic in their productivity. They produce in spurts, which looks good for a while, then flatten into unproductive valleys. Rushaholic work addicts look busy, but they usually are moving so fast they make mistakes, which then must be corrected.

I once had a solar heating system installed in my home. The company that sold and installed the system sent out a crew that was headed by a workaholic rushaholic supervisor. I had been told the installation would take up to five days to complete. Imagine my surprise at seeing the crew leave after three days. I was assured the system was installed correctly. Two weeks later, the crew was back. Not only had they installed the system incorrectly, their mistakes caused my swimming pool filter pump to break. The company then had the cost of redoing the system plus replacing my pool pump. When I spoke with the company owner, he just shook his head in frustration. "We can afford to repair it; you'd think we could afford to do it right the first time," he said.

Mistakes similar to these are common for work addicts. These things cost time, money, and emotional energy. We must also recognize the cost when work addicts burn out, as they eventually do. Experts in worker compensation claims report that stress, burnout, and psychological disease claims are double those of other worker compensation claims.

Whenever corporations promote the workaholic myth for the individual or the entire company, they are into short-term-gain thinking. Such thinking may indeed have some spectacular short-term gains, but disastrous long-term effects. Workaholism is simply not profitable for corporations.

Workaholism Is a Positive Addiction

Work addiction and fitness addiction are the two addictions we often hear described as "positive." I believe people term these two positive because they see some results: Workaholics make money, fitness addicts have good bodies. Surely, they reason, this is better than being holed up in a deserted building waiting for the next hit of coke.

First of all, the phrase "positive addiction" is a contradiction in terms. An addiction is a progressive, fatal disease. There is no such thing as an addiction that is beneficial: The very nature of addiction is that it will kill you.

A former drug addict who becomes a compulsive worker or runner has changed the content of his or her addiction, but the process stays the same. Work addicts are just as dishonest and controlling about work as drug addicts are about using.

At first, work addiction may look positive; but on closer scrutiny, it is difficult to maintain such an illusion when the work addict's personal and professional life is a shambles. Who believes workaholism is a positive addiction? The addict's family? No way. They are filled with resentment and anger at the loss of a loved one. Close acquaintances? They have the same experience as family members. Managers and some coworkers may see workaholism as positive. The media also appear to promote this addiction as positive. Many social institutions affirm workaholic styles, and therein may be the problem.

Workaholics Are Superproductive, They Get Ahead

Workaholics rarely get ahead, because the effects of their workaholic style frequently trip them up. Many workaholics make mistakes and must take extra time to cover their tracks. Often their judgment is impaired and they make wrong decisions, for which they must pay dearly. A film editor described her style as running around like a chicken without its head. She barked orders to assistants, who would take off to implement the editor's orders. Halfway through the morning she realized she had not thought through the implications of her orders; they needed a different strategy. Then she would stop her assistants in the middle of their work, make phone calls to people she really needed, and so on. The path of devastation was wide by the time the editor woke up. Coworkers put in extra time apologizing to clients and suppliers. "At the end of the day I had not only accomplished nothing, I was even further behind than if I had come to work and sat motionless for that day," she said.

Albert Einstein is an example of a man who changed the course of science and history without working like a dog. Einstein worked in his lab in the morning. He spent his afternoons sailing. He came upon the theory of relativity when, "One day while I was eating an apple, the answer appeared to me and said, 'Here I Am!'"

Perhaps some workaholics do get ahead, if getting ahead means promotions and making more money. But we must ask the cost. Many women have now spent years in the jobs they envied and couldn't have. After finally "making it," they are asking, "Is this all there is?" Making it can be hollow if you have your job but you've lost yourself and your loved ones. Workaholics have their addictions; they don't have their lives.

Workaholism Only Adversely Affects the Workaholic

Work addiction is not a private disease. Workaholics affect everyone they are in touch with—the more intimate the relationship, the greater the pain. Families of workaholics are filled with anger and resentment. They feel that they have lost a spouse, a parent. They rebel against the daily reality that they are not primary in the workaholic's life.

Workaholics are not emotionally available to their loved ones. They are often preoccupied and make promises they don't keep. These behaviors affect others. Whether they be at work or at home, the obsession with the disease takes the work addict away from others.

Those around the work addict must face their own denial and confront the ways they enable the workaholic. Spouses of workaholics say that they constantly try to second-guess the workaholics and control them, in an attempt to get time with them. These efforts usually fail, resulting in further alienation by the loved ones. A husband of a workaholic nurse said, "I let myself get caught in the web of my wife's disease. She controlled our family with her crazy schedule. I controlled her with my ultimatums. In the end we both acted the same. I felt I was a victim. I was miserable."

All addictions have a relationship component and a social component. If we could keep these diseases to ourselves, we wouldn't have the vast number of adult children of addicts and dysfunctional families we have today. Workaholics like to believe they can keep their disease a secret, but that is one of the characteristics of the disease—illusory thinking. Friends, family, organizations, and society are all affected by work addiction.

Workaholics Are Happy

A recent issue of *American Health* proclaims, "Anyone can get to the top. True winners earn a bonus: happiness." The writer defines happiness as a balanced life.[1] In hundreds of interviews with work addicts, I have heard a range of descriptions—and the word "happy" rarely occurs.

"Happy" means a feeling of well-being in the moment. Workaholics have difficulty remaining in the here and now. They are in the past or in the future, either avoiding work or doing work.

Work addicts feel driven by the compulsion to work. They also feel empty. Neither driveness nor emptiness is happiness.

Some work addicts say they will feel happy when their tasks are accomplished. Of course, the work is never done. Thus happiness dangles like the proverbial carrot. It is only the next project away.

The myth that workaholics are happy is like the myth that workaholics are productive. Both are illusions of an addictive society that would have us blind ourselves to what is really going on.

"Happy?" laughed an acquaintance who recently began her recovery from work addiction. "In my family there was 'good,' 'productive,' 'work,' and 'make us proud.' I never heard 'happy.' I felt happy the day I finally said, 'I'm powerless over this disease in my life.' And then it was such a fleeting feeling I didn't know what it was!"

Some workaholics may earn fabulous salaries, a few get to the top, some just make it through another day. Few are truly happy.

2. Four Types of Work Addicts

I believe that our information and awareness about work addiction is so elementary that we have the naive belief that a work addict is just a person who works too much. Because, as Twelve-Step groups tell us, addictions are "cunning, baffling, patient, and powerful," they can change their form. I have discovered at least four forms of work addiction. I am sure there are more but here are the four forms I find most prevalent: the compulsive worker, the binge worker, the closet worker, and the work anorexic.

The Compulsive Worker

The compulsive worker is the form we know best. This is the generic workaholic—the person who is simply driven to work all the time. This type is the one on which our stereotype of the workaholic was originally based.

These work addicts are the first to arrive at work and the last to leave. They take work with them on vacation—if they take vacations. They rarely agree to vacations until the last minute. They would never plan ahead, because "you never know what will come up at work." Compulsive workers usually work when they are not required to do so by bosses or company deadlines.

Compulsion and perfectionism go hand-in-hand with these workaholics. A secretary in an oil company related that she often had Friday deadlines that she would meet by Wednesday. However, the Wednesday deadline did not give her slack time until Friday. No, she used the extra two days to rework and rework the project until it was "perfect." By Friday she felt exhausted and behind in her other work. Then on Monday this process would begin over again. Although this pattern was nerve-racking and harmful for the secretary, she continued in it regardless of the negative consequences.

Compulsive work addicts are dishonest. Inevitably, others begin to notice their pattern. Soon they lie about work. They secret projects away. They hide their stash. They lash out in anger when confronted by loved ones. They feel misunderstood. They make promises: "If you could only understand. Let me finish this one thing and I'll have time for you." However, the chief characteristic of the compulsive work addict is that when one thing is finished there is another equally urgent piece that must be done. Work is god for the compulsive worker, and nothing gets in the way of this god.

Tunnel vision characterizes compulsives. They see only one thing, and that is the task before them followed by a parade of other tasks. They are tricky to live with, because often these work projects are done for the family—to ensure a better life. Many codependents of compulsive workers feel conflicted. They observe the addict saying, "I don't like it either, but I do it for our life, for you." This attitude is always a trap for the family and serves to keep them away from the addict's supply, which is his or her work.

Compulsive work addicts are different from the other types in that they are usually obvious. Although dishonest about their addiction, and hostile when confronted, still they are easy to detect because they work constantly.

The Binge Worker

Binge workers share the characteristics of compulsives, with an important exception. Intensity, not constancy, is the mark of their addiction. Binge workers are like binge drinkers or binge eaters. They will go along seemingly "normal," and suddenly they will go on a binge of working. They may go days without sleep. Indeed, they are so focused on the work in front of them that they lose all track of time.

Jack is a binge worker. He develops management seminars for a government agency. He has a good reputation in a field where performance is always evaluated by the participants in his seminars. His job is secure and he has received promotions routinely. He is not a newcomer to the field. He is a pro. Jack is married, with two teenage sons. Although Jack comes from an alcoholic family (his father died of alcoholism when Jack was eighteen), he believes he has not had any problem with addictions—that is, until recently. Increasingly, Jack is binging on work.

He goes along fine, and then suddenly he finds himself with an overpowering need to stay at work and "finish up a few things." He loses all track of time and attention when he goes on the binge. Sometimes the binges go on for a week or ten days. The longest was two weeks. During that time Jack worked with only four hours of sleep a night. Some nights he slept on a mat on his office floor. He describes the binge as a period when he leaves himself and becomes obsessed with work. This obsession results in numbness in all other areas of his life. He does not take care of his physical or psychological needs. His office is littered with remnants of take-out food; he looks gray around his jowls; his family thinks of him as "gone."

Jack is frightened by the increasing frequency of these binges. Initially, they occurred once or twice a year. Now he is binging a few days several times a month. Also, Jack says he is "good for nothing" after a work binge. He is like a drunk with a hangover.

Indeed, Jack is suffering a hangover. The only difference between him and his alcoholic father is that Jack's substance of choice is work. Like the binge drinker, Jack "saves it up" and "ties one on" in a few days of working. Work is medication for him. It numbs him to his feelings, to his questions, perhaps to his unresolved pain. He has become so busy with binges and the aftermath of binges that he has no time for the rest of his life. His family, which was understanding in the beginning, is now worried that Jack is on a collision course with illness if he continues in this way.

A few months after recording Jack's story, I heard that he was hospitalized for exhaustion and remained out of work for two months.

Binging may be difficult to detect because most of us have periods when we need to put in extra effort or stay longer. But when binging becomes the pattern of work in one's life or in the expectation of an organization, then the addiction to work has clicked in. Consequences as dire as Jack's are inevitable if the pattern is not interrupted.

The Closet Worker

If you have ever known a closet eater, you will understand the closet work addict. In the open—that is, in the places where he or she can be observed—a closet eater eats appropriately. Mysteriously, however, the person continues to gain weight; or, if the person binges and purges, he or she may even lose weight. Closet work addicts operate similarly.

Closet work addicts often have a niggling awareness that something is dysfunctional about their work style. Their families and loved ones may also be "on" to them, and ask that they look at their addiction. The closet worker may make halfway promises to cut back or to regulate work, none of which they are able to keep.

There are at least two types of closet work addicts. Type one literally hides work and then does it when there is little likelihood of being discovered. These are the people who sequester files in gym bags or beach bags, only to whip them out when companions are off enjoying themselves. Hal was such an addict. He is in recovery now, so he can look back on what he calls his "Hilarious Hawaiian Holiday."

After years of no vacations, Hal and his wife, Karen, were finally going to Hawaii. But Hal, a metallurgist, was panicky at the thought of being away from work, and, "Of course, wouldn't you know, the two weeks I was to be gone we were testing a new product." Hal had promised Karen this vacation for over a year. He didn't dare go back on his agreement, yet he was desperate to be in on activities back at work. Consequently, every chance he got, Hal found ways to be away from Karen so he could study files and place phone calls back to the office. Hal and Karen would pull up to a grocery: "You go in, I'll just wait in the car," Hal would say, his fingers itching to get to his file. He would encourage Karen to do things on her own, not because he supported her independence, but because he was in the grip of his addiction.

Hal described the relief he felt the day he announced he was going to play golf. He knew Karen had no interest in golf. He went to the golf course, but instead of playing nine holes, he used the phone in the clubhouse to call his office. He believed if he could just get sufficient time on the phone with his office staff, he would be able to participate freely in the remainder of his vacation. Notice Hal's bargaining with his disease. Unfortunately, the phone call was not the end of Hal's involvement. Hal's staff had a whole new series of problems to run by him, and what had appeared to be the final push to satisfy his compulsion was the beginning of further conniving for secret liaisons with work and office.

Hal entered treatment when Karen confronted him with the fact that she believed he was having an affair! His behavior had become so secretive that Karen figured he was seeing someone else. Today, Hal laughingly says, "I was having an affair all right—only my mistress was work." On a more serious note, Hal said he woke up to the fact that no amount of contact with work was going to be enough. He saw himself as powerless, and he was ashamed of how silly he looked hiding files in beach bags and casing out every hotel for the nearest "safe" phone. Hal first admitted his powerlessness to himself and second to Karen. This admission was step one in a program of recovery Hal does every day.

Type two closet work addicts also sequester work, but they have developed a more sophisticated con. Type two addicts may have recognized that their work styles are out of control, and they appear to be taking steps to deal with it. But within their attempts at reform, they hide their stash.

Linda, editor of a women's magazine, had asked her husband, George, to support her in dealing with her workaholism. For over two years, Linda had been working weekends. She was rarely available for social or family activities. The nature of her business was such that she felt she accomplished more work at home on weekends, but even she was beginning to notice the toll this practice was taking on her marriage. Thus Linda entered into an agreement with George. On Saturday morning, before leaping out of bed, Linda would say out loud to George the three—and only three—tasks she was going to do for that day. This process worked for a few months, and then Linda noticed that within each of the three tasks she found a way to add other things. For example, task one was, "Review an author's manuscript." Not only did Linda review the manuscript; while she was at it she checked the author's contract, had a look at publicity plans, and so on. Before task one was completed, she had managed to squeeze in a slew of other activities—all justified under a particular author's name.

Addictions are cunning; they are patient. Linda had tricked herself and her husband into believing she was facing her workaholism when, in fact, she was getting trickier. Like Hal, Linda had the experience that no amount of promising solved the problem. She felt increasingly incongruent as she played a "game" with George on Saturday mornings, mapping out her three tasks, only to fall into her old patterns when she got to the tasks. Now, in her recovery, she knows that breaking promises is a trigger that throws her back into her workaholism.

The Work Anorexic

If you are someone who thinks dualistically, you have decided that the "cure" for workaholism is not working at all! However, dualistic thinking is a characteristic of the addictive process, and the avoidance of work is as much a compulsion of workaholism as overworking is. The work anorexic's theme song is, "I'm darn good at what I do, but I seldom do it."[1]

Margaret is a work anorexic. She comes from the nation that invented the concept of hard work, Germany. Margaret first realized she was addicted to work through obsession with not working at a meeting with her friend, Bert. Bert was sharing his problem with eating, and he said that he experienced not eating as the other side of overeating. In both instances, he was focused on food and overly preoccupied with body image.

Margaret studied art and German language. As an artist, she thinks the myths about the unusual lifestyles and work styles of artists have fed her work anorexia. "I believed artists were not supposed to meet deadlines or to work a normal eight-hour day. I felt the all-night binges of work and rushing at the last minute were part of my identity as an artist. Besides, it was only at the last minute that I could get a good concentration." Margaret said she felt a fascination with pushing at the last minute. She said it enabled her to feel different, unique. Margaret cannot work an eight-hour day. She can only work under pressure.

Margaret sees herself as someone who is addicted to avoiding. She avoids at every level of her life—work, friendships, even physical needs—"Sometimes I don't even brush my teeth." Her avoidance, she feels, is related to her perfectionism and to an internal belief that she should make no mistakes.

Margaret will use anything to procrastinate. She says, "I even go to the Workaholics Anonymous meetings to avoid work. I run away from what I need to do at home by going to a meeting!"

Margaret's perfectionism leads to her procrastination. Her procrastination results in guilt, and guilt immobilizes her. Immobility is a way to avoid intimacy with herself, her projects, and with other people. Margaret is in extreme pain over this problem. I can see the pain in her eyes as she tells her story. She says: "I always left things half-done. I prepared a lot so I could get to work. In preparing, I read and read what others had written instead of getting to the part where I write down what I need to say. I had no intimacy with my own thoughts. In my head I had expectations of what I thought others wanted me to do. I fought that, and I realized it kept me busy fighting something I created in my mind."

Last, Margaret finds that her lack of intimacy feeds another aspect of her work anorexia. She has no boundaries; therefore she never knows when she has worked enough, or when she has written enough. She experiences her life as filled with drama. It takes her twelve semesters instead of eight to finish her degree. She uses schedules to push herself to finish projects, because she can't regulate her activity internally. She is at the whim of expectations external to herself. She uses schedules and last-minute deadlines to push herself to perform. And although she finally does her work, she loses herself, because something outside herself mounts a pressure she obeys unthinkingly.

The pressure, drama, crisis — and, yes, romance — of pushing the last-minute limit is the one high Margaret has in her life, and it leaves her exhausted and confused after the deadline is met. She goes through life like a person who slips under the gate just as it is closing. Her life is a "Whew! I made it," but her disease prevents her from asking an essential question: Is this the life I want? The process of slipping under the gate last is so engrossing that Margaret is not sure she wants what is on the other side. This is the insidious aspect of workaholism. We are so caught up in the race, we cease asking if we desire the prize. For the workaholic, the prize frequently is external. You get "something" at the loss of yourself.

The work addicts' disease has many facets, sometimes manifesting in compulsive work, sometimes in work anorexia. I know work addicts who move between all four types with ease. They just about get their binging addressed when they slide into closet working. As with any addictive process, it is important to understand what aspect of work addiction is causing you the worst trouble in your life now. Meeting that aspect, one step at a time, is the beginning of the healing process.

3. Characteristics of Workaholics

It is clear from the foregoing information that addiction to work is indeed cunning and baffling. Not only are there various types of workaholics, the characteristics of the disease may manifest differently in different people. I want to describe the characteristics of workaholism in the individual, but I do this with a certain amount of trepidation.

I am leery of lists of characteristics. In our trickiness, we go through these lists mentally clicking off "That's me, that's not me." Then the list-makers tell us how many "that's me's" we need to be "one." Frequently, we use the list as an external referent. It tells us; we don't check out internally whether the description fits. Ultimately, however, we have to ask ourselves if our lives are becoming unmanageable in relation to our busyness, rushing, and working. If from inside the answer is "yes," we may need to face the possibility that we have an addiction to work.

Here are the primary characteristics of workaholics:

- multiple addictions
- denial
- self-esteem problems
- external referenting
- inability to relax
- obsessiveness

These characteristics and the following stories came to me from workaholics themselves and from the material generated by the first Workaholics Anonymous groups in the United States. Whether one, two, or most of the characteristics fit is not the issue. The issue is this: Is your life increasingly unmanageable in relation to work, busyness, rushing, or caring?

Multiple Addictions

I have never met a person with only one addiction. Anyone who attends an Alcoholics Anonymous (AA) meeting in this country understands this — the room is filled with smoke and the coffeepot is perking! As Anne Wilson Schaef says, "Most recovering addicts find that we must face-off with the addiction that is giving us the most trouble. After we face it we find another addiction waiting to be worked."

For example, many work addicts find that their work addiction goes hand in hand with a relationship addiction. They cannot bear to disappoint others or to say "no" to excessive demands, for fear of others' disapproval. Perhaps as ACOAs (adult children of alcoholics and dysfunctional families) they constantly seek approval and affirmation, which they receive through work. Some people who are working a solid program of recovery from their chemical addiction may now be working with the same intensity with which they abused alcohol. Or workaholics, in their pain, may find themselves "taking the edge off" a hard day by having too many alcoholic drinks.

I find that the three usual backup addictions of workaholics are money, food, and relationships. Often, people fly among these three: not taking time to carefully consider shaky business deals because they promise big bucks; overworking and then nurturing themselves by overeating; prolonging work or staying late to please a boss or coworker. In each of these instances, the backup or secondary addiction kicks in to justify or blunt the primary addiction to work.

Ultimately, we have to address what Schaef calls the underlying addictive process. Workaholism gives us many opportunities to understand both our inner dynamics and the dynamics of the disease. If work is the common denominator in all the areas where one's life is getting crazy, that is the addiction to be faced; but we should not congratulate ourselves that we have licked the addictive process! Addictions are a progressive process and so, too, is recovery. For example, we cannot recover from our overwork and continue in our food and relationship addictions without still being in a life-threatening situation. Facing our addictive process, whatever the specific addiction, is a lifelong task.

Denial

Every addiction rests squarely on denial. Denial is the first defense of the addictive process. Without denial, addictions crumble. When you break through your denial and acknowledge you are a workaholic, you are 50 percent into recovery. Unless you confront denial, it is useless to deal with any other steps to recovery.

The workaholic's denial is one of the trickiest of all denials, because there appears to be no denial. Workaholism is one of the few addictions people boast about. They boast socially, publicly, and to the media. In print we see such stories as, "Ten women under 30 who made a million. They work hard, they play hard, they're workaholics and love it." It is extremely difficult to admit your addiction—especially if you have trouble with your boundaries and identity, as work addicts do—in the face of societal pressure telling you work addiction is positive.

There are several dimensions to the work addicts' denial. Some stay in denial by the process of comparison. They say, "I know I'm a workaholic, but it's better than a lot of other things I could be. We all have to die of something. It may as well be work." Another technique is the trade-off. "Sure I'm a workaholic, but look at the benefits I've received. As a result of my working, rushing, caring I've . . ." (you fill in the blanks). The illusion in this denial is that none of these benefits would come without the workaholism. A third form of denial is that workaholics admit their addiction, but they do not see it as dangerous for them. This form is the scariest of all. One of the characteristics of the addictive disease is a progressive loss of judgment, a lowered ability to make decisions that are in our best interests. The disease progresses in us whether we are aware of it or not.

The workaholic denies, and the family supports the denial. When loved ones turn away from their awareness of the effects of the workaholic on them, they enter the addictive process with the work addict. They are also in pain in relation to the workaholic, but they refuse to acknowledge their pain to themselves or their loved one. They mimic the denial of the workaholic in their own complaints: "He's a great provider, but we never see him"; or, "I suppose she could be doing worse things than working all the time, like running around with other men"; or this line from a Glasbergen cartoon, "Do you have any perfume that smells like a desk? My husband is a workaholic."

Self-Esteem Problems

Work addicts have either overinflated or underinflated perceptions of themselves. They truly have a hard time seeing themselves honestly and accepting themselves for who they are. They fluctuate between seeing themselves as the most capable people or the most incapable. Consequently, they will make promises they can't fulfill (based on illusions of capability), only to feel embarrassed and shameful later. Or they bypass projects they could easily handle (based on illusions of worthlessness) and then punish themselves for lost opportunities.

Problems with self-esteem lead to a high degree of dishonesty. Believing that people will not accept them for who they are, workaholics tend to exaggerate their achievements and rarely mention their failures.

I experienced this aspect of the disease when I was interviewing a nurse for a job in a clinic. Her resumé was sterling. She had apparently been a success from the beginning. After hiring her, however, the clinic discovered she lacked some rudimentary nursing skills and her personality was horrible. She compensated by working twice as hard as everyone else, but her rushing and busyness resulted in knocked-over bottles, botched appointments, and a host of errors that had to be cleaned up behind her. Needless to say she was fired, and I feel sure the clinic that fired her does not appear on her new resumé. I can only guess how many previous jobs aren't there either!

It is important to recognize that not only was the nurse dishonest in her resumé, she lives in an organizational milieu that expects people to promote themselves as flawless. What job counselor ever said, "Show the way you've grown through both success and failure"? The nurse was doing exactly what she believed was acceptable in a workaholic culture. Many work addicts report that they were only praised for success, not growth.

Many people in the addictions field point to self-esteem as the central issue in the predisposition to addictions. I don't believe there is one primary cause of addictions, and I do see self-esteem as a key struggle in recovery. Workaholics, like every addict, eventually have to face into the pain that work numbs. Addictions take us out of touch with our lives, and we disengage from every aspect of our knowing and feeling. The workaholic's self-esteem issue is the fear that there may be no one inside worth knowing or, worse, there may be no one at all.

Regaining a true sense of self is one of the risks of recovery from workaholism, and it is also one of its promises.

External Referenting

External referenting is looking outside yourself for clues to how to act, what to feel. People who grow up in dysfunctional families spend inordinate amounts of time focused outside themselves. This is necessary in order to survive. Sometimes your very life depends upon anticipating the actions of the addict in your family. Unfortunately, this basic training of childhood is the perfect setup for work addiction.

Years before I decided to write a book about work addiction, I noticed a curious trait in a friend, a chief executive officer (CEO) in a large company. I would meet him for lunch and ask him how he was, and he responded by telling me what he was doing! Later, I realized workaholics are the addicts who will tell you what they do in response to how they are.

Accomplishments are the workaholic's primary external means of knowing who they are. Because they judge themselves by their accomplishments, they have the illusion they must always be doing something worthwhile in order to feel good about themselves. Of course, "worthwhile" accomplishments are visible (to others). Therefore a work addict would resist thirty minutes of solitude, even if it meant being more effective at work, because solitude could not be observed. Or the workaholic will take thirty minutes of solitude and find a way, in conversation with coworkers, to justify why solitude enabled them to work harder than before. For the work addict, every activity and nonactivity must justify itself in terms of its support of work, otherwise it has no reason for being—just as the workaholic believes he or she has no reason to be without the justification of work.

Since feeling good is related to task accomplishment, workaholics are often facing depression. They usually assign themselves more work than they can hope to do, so they inevitably disappoint themselves and those who count on them. My friend Jackie says she discovered a way to avoid even the feelings of disappointment. She moved on to another task so quickly that she didn't have time to feel anything!

Work addicts are inveterate list makers. The list serves as the ultimate external referent: If it is not on the list, it doesn't exist and it doesn't get attention. Workaholics' styles of list making are truly mind-boggling.

Richard has a master list done by categorics: phone calls, correspondence, projects (long-term and short-term), follow-up, new contacts, personal, personal-family, personal-friends, and so on. Everyday he constructs a daily list from the master list. New things keep getting added to the master list, and some things that don't get done on the daily list have to be carried over to the following day. (Tired yet?) When I spoke to Richard he had eight months of lists he carried in a file everywhere he went. He felt obsessed with going back over each list and never throwing one away until everything on the list was done.

"Oh, I can do Richard one better," said Elizabeth, a book agent. "If an item does not appear on my list, it does not get done—no matter what. If it does appear, it gets done—even if I know in the moment that activity is useless or inappropriate. For example, I will not exercise or spend time with my kids unless I see '2 P.M.–4 P.M.—time for kids' on the list. The list dictates my life. Without it, I would be lost." "But what about your kids?" I asked. "What if they don't want to spend from 2 o'clock to 4 o'clock with you? What about their needs and schedules?" "Too bad," Elizabeth shrugged. "If they want time with their mom, this is when it is."

I left this encounter feeling pensive. In the era of two-career families and single parents, we've heard a lot about spending quality time with children, making every moment count, especially when there are not very many moments. Elizabeth's style seems to have abandoned quality altogether. Her kids are just another item to be checked off the list. She may not be present to them; they may not be present to her. In

the end they just "did it." I began to see the power of workaholism as a generational disease. Elizabeth's children were
learning a rudimentary skill of the dysfunctional family:
external referenting of life by the list.

Inability to Relax

I noted earlier that workaholics run on hyper-adrenaline. The
adrenaline is a major contributor to the inability to relax.
Even when the work addict is ready for sleep, the system may
not be able to turn off.

Work addicts have an endless array of tasks, and they
always feel the need to get just a few more done. Since work is
the "stash," when present tasks are done, there are a few more.

I knew a housewife who felt discomfort in face-to-face
conversation. She felt others would see through her, and she
felt unworthy. Still, she was social and enjoyed company.
When guests came over, she busied herself in the kitchen
while they talked. After dinner she was the first to jump up
and clean the dishes. When her guests offered to help with the
dishes, she demurred. She was comfortable visiting people in
the kitchen so long as she had something to do. So she dried
silverware, folded napkins, cleaned out cracks on appliances.
Others protested she should quit, relax, and join them in the
living room, but she set it up so that rarely happened and people eventually drifted into the kitchen when they desired her
company. Of course, she made it difficult for them to confront
her because she was always serving them. All she ever knew
about her compulsion to work and her inability to relax was
that she needed "something" between herself and other people. And she fiercely guarded that something all her life.

Procrastinators and work anorexics have difficulty relaxing, although you would never know it by looking at them.
They are in constant internal turmoil. They feel resentment
about having to complete tasks. They cannot concentrate on

the task at hand. They punish themselves by avoiding work and then beating up on themselves for procrastinating—not a very relaxing place to be!

Many workaholics operate in a constant crisis mode (usually because they schedule themselves for more than they can handle); consequently, they feel the uproar of the crisis, but they rarely experience their true emotions. Work addicts cannot just sit and be. They say repeatedly, in almost every interview, that it is simply too terrifying to just sit and be. Some work addicts acknowledge that if they relaxed, they might feel emotions they wish to avoid. Others have a terror of the void, an emptiness too fearful to explore. Whatever it is they fear, they readily acknowledge that work keeps these feelings down and inaccessible on a daily basis.

Many workaholic businesses use the crisis orientation as an excuse for a corporate inability to relax. In these companies, people are always dropping what they are doing to respond to a seemingly more critical need. A consultant who deals with workaholic companies observed that her most difficult challenge is to show managers that they do not need to react if they have planned their business. They become so frightened about knowing what they really need to do that they would rather close their eyes and put out fires.

The inability to relax does not come from work itself, but from incessant work and the way we work. When work is a fix it carries a burden it cannot sustain. Work cannot give us an identity. It cannot *make* us happy. When we expect our work to do things for us that we are not willing to do for ourselves, we become exhausted. More is not better where work is concerned.

Healthy people are enlivened and stimulated by work. They don't expect work to make them whole. They are whole and they choose to work. Sure, such people are tired at the end of a day, but not with the disabling exhaustion of the work addict.

The inability to relax is a serious symptom for the workaholic, because it signals that the physical and psychological systems are running on overload. Like an out-of-control train streaking down a mountainside, the brakes are of no avail. Only a crash will stop it.

Obsessiveness

To be obsessive is to be driven. Many work addicts describe themselves as being on automatic pilot. They move through a day, but they are not actually in the driver's seat. One of the symptoms indicating the disease is worsening is the sense that something besides yourself has taken over. An accompanying signal is that you think of work constantly—in bed, in the shower, during conversations, while watching TV, and while driving.

Obsessiveness is not particular about its object. You can be obsessively perfectionistic about the form of a letter or doing good works. Carol, a nurse, directed her obsessive serving toward poor migrant workers. At the time her obsessive serving peaked, she was on four boards and was the chairperson of three of them. She now sees that her workaholism got hooked because she believed it was for a good cause. Raised as a "good Christian," Carol looked askance at those who worked hard only to accumulate wealth for themselves. But the migrant program was not for her advancement—in fact, she took a cut in pay—but for those more needy than she was.

Carol left her quarters at 8 A.M. and returned at midnight. She would use the toilet only twice in that period—once before she left and when she returned at night. She drove from migrant camp to migrant camp and ate only candy bars and chocolate shakes. She existed on sugar. In addition, Carol was in a crazy relationship—they spent their "free" time fixing up their rental house in order to leave a better place for the next person, and also to avoid dealing with their conflict with each other.

By the time Carol quit the migrant project she was physically strung out and barely able to provide the services she had come to do. She went back to her hometown and took a job at a hospital, where she worked sixty hours a week. The sixty hours felt like a vacation after the migrant project. She thought she was doing well until one evening, after a typical day at the hospital, Carol chopped off her finger while fixing supper. This accident gave her an enforced two weeks off work, a period that turned her around.

Carol knew something was wrong with her life. During her time off, she obsessively searched for an answer. She read compulsively, looking for a cure — first New Age, then crystals and herbs, then addiction books. "I 'drank books' the way any drunk does alcohol. I had been obsessively sick, now I was going to get well; but I was doing 'well' the way I did sick," said Carol.

Carol's realization that she was trying to recover in an obsessive manner was a key point in her recovery. She has faced her obsessiveness and now does wellness with more gentleness.

Obsessiveness can extend to areas beyond work, as Carol's story exemplifies. I knew a man who had an excessive desire to understand everything in his life and in his family's life. He would spend hours in self-examination, asking himself, "Why did I do that? Why do I feel this way? Why are others acting as they do?" He exhausted himself and others, not to mention how disrespectful he was in his incessant poking into everyone's motivation.

Obsessiveness can endanger your life. Carol lost a finger, a daily reminder to her about her disease. Workaholics are always trading stories about missed train stops, driving past highway exits, driving into the rear ends of stopped cars due to preoccupation with thoughts about work or whatever it is they are focused on. Some use these events to wake up to the reality of work addiction in their lives; others are too obsessed with understanding why it happened to use the event to change their lives.

Other Characteristics

The foregoing six characteristics are reported to me by most work addicts. In addition, work addicts share other characteristics:

- dishonesty
- self-centeredness
- isolation
- control
- perfectionism
- piles and files
- lack of intimacy
- self-abuse
- physical and psychological problems
- spiritual bankruptcy

Dishonesty

In order to protect their supply, work addicts lie. They lie about how much they work, and how often they work. As closet workers, they hide work. They are dishonest with themselves and with others. Like denial, dishonesty is essential in keeping up the facade that says "I'm OK," when actually their lives are crumbling down around them.

Self-Centeredness

Work addicts have an exaggerated sense of the importance of their projects. Children of workaholic parents recall that nothing interfered with a parent's work. Their work came first, and all other plans gave way. Addicts will do anything to get to their fix, including running over loved ones and breaking promises. Workaholics prefer jobs with important titles or the opportunity to control others. They think of others as servants, not peers. Their self-centeredness expresses itself in acting superior, finding fault with experts, and so on.

Careaholics persist in the illusion that without them no one would be served. It is always a shock to the careaholic to see others pitch in and carry on when they leave. Of course, the self-centeredness keeps us in the disease; and while it fosters our workaholism, it prevents us from attaining true self-love in which we are at the center but not at the expense of others or ourselves.

Isolation

Workaholics tend to remove themselves from others in several ways. First, the obsession with work, with rushing, and busyness is inherently isolating because others cannot keep up with the addict. Like an airplane on an aborted landing, work addicts touch down and take off again. Second, as others become concerned about the workaholic, the workaholic begins removing himself or herself from those who may accumulate enough information to confront the problem. Finally, work addicts work alone when others decide to limit their hours or say "no" to excessive demands.

Control

The illusion of control dies slowly for work addicts, because control pervades so many aspects of their lives. They have the illusion that they can control the amount they work and the intensity. They believe they can control how others see them. Managers and workaholic organizations attempt to control workers, and they assume that a workaholic approach will ultimately control productivity. Time management may be the height of the control illusion, for addicts truly believe there is a way to handle time so they have more of it!

As work addiction progresses, the attempts at control become greater. The work addict's inner life is in chaos, so the efforts to hold it together must be made externally. Giving up the illusion of control is extremely difficult, but doing so is a key building block of recovery.

Perfectionism

Perfectionism is hooked by the illusion that "I am not human." Workaholics have trouble with humanness. Humans need sleep, make mistakes, have feelings and needs. This is not a description of a workaholic. Perfectionistic bosses and co-workers are candidates for burnout because they believe their efforts and their control of themselves and other people will make things turn out the way they want it. They are frequently disappointed when things don't go perfectly.

I knew a perfectionistic manager whose perfection made him a basket case in relation to his staff. He had certain ways of doing things, and he taught those to his staff. He believed in delegating, so he gave away a lot of responsibility. Unfortunately, his staff didn't do tasks perfectly; they made mistakes. When he observed the mistakes he said, "See, if I trust them with the work, they don't do it right and I have to do it over. Therefore, why delegate to them in the first place? I only end up doing the work anyway." The result of his perfectionistic attitude was that he precipitated more mistakes on the part of his staff because they had fewer opportunities to learn by doing. Also, he did his own work and a large part of their work because it was the only way he could guarantee it would be done perfectly—that is, his way.

Perhaps perfectionists are the only ones who work themselves to death while those they hired to help stand by watching!

Piles and Files

All addicts have their stash, and workaholics are no exception. Piles and files are two common stashes for work addicts.

I once did a simple test with a workshop group. I said, "If I came into your house and cleared out your liquor cabinet, pitched all the bottles and you'd never see them again, how would you react?" Most (not the alcoholics!) replied they would be upset, but it would not be the end of their lives. "Well," I said, "If I came into your office and I went to your filing cabinet and I pitched your files and you'd never see them again, how would you feel?" The majority gasped. Several said, "I would panic and immediately begin to scheme where and how I could get copies of those files." Said others, now getting more honest, "I could not live without my files."

The files represent a continuing supply of work, projects upon projects for years to come. You never get ahead; and when you finish one, another is waiting. An organizational consultant who helps work addicts deal with their personal productivity told me, "Peace of mind is so uncomfortable." She says she deals with a client who cannot get his desk organized. Nothing seems to be working with this man. One day he did get his desk organized, and he let slip to the consultant, "Oops! Now that my desk is in order I have to face into me!" Work addicts can stay busy for years with seemingly important pieces of paper, shuffling them around from place to place, all in the service of staying out of touch with their own internal processes.

Jeri lives among skyscrapers of piles at home and at the office. She believes that if she puts things away she won't do them, so she needs them constantly in her line of vision or they'll be forgotten. This method confounds her: "I end up with piles everywhere. Then I don't see the things on the bottom. I put the important work on my desk, but then the other stuff gets put on top. Finally, my urgent work is placed on the center of my desk. I know to do it first, but even that pile is half-done."

We see the same pattern in Jeri's apartment. For a year and a half she has lived among unpacked boxes. She realizes that her control is in her belief she can arrange her apartment exactly the way she wants it. Since this goal is unattainable, she refuses to go even halfway to create a comfortable place for herself. "The boxes stand, always handy to take me away from myself. I never say, 'Today I'll unpack half a box.' It's all or nothing. It's a big, unmanageable chunk that can't be done, and it is constantly there to remind me."

Jeri's apartment looks the same as it did a year and a half earlier. Friends are waiting for invitations to dinner, but Jeri is too ashamed for them to see the apartment. Besides, where would they sit? A procrastinator at home, she is a binge worker at the office. When the pressure is on, she closes her door and works five hours straight to clear her desk. Jeri spends enormous energy beating herself up for not doing it right; then, exhausted mentally and emotionally, she has no energy to take the steps that would relieve her of this disease process.

Files and piles aren't the addictive process itself. They are the tools a work addict uses to stay in the addiction. Given our lifestyle in the United States, we'll always have "stuff" that needs attending. When we believe we can and should control these things, we're in trouble. There's some truth to the saying, "We are what we do." When what we do is live preoccupied with our files and piles, we become just as lifeless as these objects.

Lack of Intimacy

It is easy to see how work addicts use working, rushing, and busyness to stay out of touch with themselves and with others. In the previous example, the man with the cluttered desk didn't want to clear his desk for fear he'd have to face himself. In the same way, workaholics use work as the means to avoid intimacy with self.

It is not true, however, that work addicts are loners hiding behind stacks of papers. Some work addicts are sociable; they have acquaintances, but frequently their social contacts are really work contacts. Or, as a recent article in *Fortune* put it, "All socializing by the workaholic generation is for the purpose of making future business contacts."[1] This type of socializing supports work addiction and prevents true intimacy. Workaholics use work to avoid intimacy. They stay busy with interesting projects and never meet the challenges of knowing another or being known themselves. True intimacy requires giving up the illusion of control — a difficult task for the work addict.

Work addiction affects at least three levels of intimacy. On the first level, workaholics are out of touch with self. They have no awareness of feelings, only emotional poverty. On the second level, workaholics have no genuine connection with loved ones, be they spouses, children, or friends. They may meet on the run, or have some superficial sharing, but there is not a closeness born of time to know and be known. On the third level, workaholics have no intimacy with work itself. The work — which is the thing they are losing their life in — becomes an object to satisfy the addiction, not a source of liveliness.

Self-Abuse

The workaholic lifestyle is self-abusive. It is emotionally abusive, because it results in cycles of internal messages based on comparison: "I'm no good," "I'm not enough," and so on. It is physically abusive, because it sets people into a pace that eventually has to result in burnout. At all levels, work addiction is destructive; and the destruction ripples out from the addict to family, organization, and eventually the world.

Physical and Psychological Problems

As the workaholic's disease progresses, it is inevitable that various physical and psychological symptoms appear. The danger, however, is that workaholics are so out of touch with their own physical processes that they require a serious disease like a heart attack to get their attention.

In this generation we have seen the rise of exotic fatigue diseases and swift killers. *Karoshi,* or "death from overwork," is a disturbing phenomenon in Japan. The disease, which is linked to too much work and not enough play, typically affects men who put in twelve- to sixteen-hour days over many years. The victims, usually between the ages of forty and fifty, have no previous health problems. They apparently just work themselves to death. Two-thirds of the deaths are from brain hemorrhages, one-third from myocardial infarction. According to Japan's Ministry of Health and Welfare, *karoshi* may account for 10 percent of all deaths of working men in Japan, making it the second-largest killer of this population.[2]

In our country, we see the rise of chronic fatigue syndrome, variously called Epstein-Barr and Yuppie's Disease, because it tends to affect upwardly mobile professional women in their twenties and thirties. Characterized by swollen glands, fever, sore joints, and overpowering fatigue, these chronic viral syndromes can last for months, even years. Researchers are still puzzled about the causes of chronic fatigue. However, a recent research study found striking similarities between the characteristics of chronic cocaine abuse and fatigue syndrome, suggesting that addictive process disorders may result in chronic fatigue.[3] Certainly, the constant stress of workaholism suppresses the immune system, which is then ripe for viral infection.

In addition to chronic fatigue and death from overwork, work addicts also experience such stress-related ills as ulcers, gastro-intestinal problems, backaches, difficulty sleeping, headaches, and high blood pressure. Even with such severe symptoms, work addicts ignore their pain. A woman confided: "We workaholics don't feel pain. I would not have told you I hurt. I was so high on my adrenaline I felt great. It was only when my body gave out that I began to feel the pain, and I ignored the symptoms for months, thinking it was just psychosomatic and I could push through the pain."

Psychologically, work addicts experience progressive deadening of their feelings. Some workaholics may have used their disease since childhood to compensate for the pain of the dysfunctional family. Thus the separation from feelings is longstanding. Said one ACOA (Adult Children of Alcoholics) airline mechanic: "I used busyness starting at age eight as a way to avoid my crazy family. I cleaned house, joined clubs, had hobbies, pleased my parents and school authorities — anything to keep at bay the terror of living in my mixed-up family. Even now, I don't allow myself to feel satisfaction at my success. I move immediately on to something else."

Other work addicts exhibit severe mood swings, fluctuating between manic euphoria and severe depression. This moodiness is often related to work styles. Euphoric workers work hard, like binge workers, and their productively goes in spurts. Depressed workers resemble anorexic workers. They procrastinate and can hardly get moving at all.

Most workaholics suffer from forgetfulness. Research on substance and process addiction has shown that memory loss is a characteristic of the disease. A recovering workaholic observed that if he had counted the time he spent searching for his keys, creating uproars over lost papers (which "mysteriously" reappeared on his desk), and sending secretaries on errands to buy replacements for lost items that were eventually found, he would have another lifetime to live.

Not only do work addicts lose things, they forget appointments and commitments. They forget ideas and plans. Addicts are people who make promises they cannot keep or do not intend to keep. They say "yes" when they mean "no," so they promptly forget things they agree to do. The workaholics' hectic pace is such that they cannot possibly meet all the commitments they set for themselves. They usually feel they are playing catch-up. This results in irritability, fits of temper, feelings of being misunderstood, and a tendency to suffer.

The work addict's life gradually unravels physically and emotionally. Family members may become immune to the addict. In their denial, they believe, "That's just the way Mom or Dad is." In truth, a disease process is gaining ground in the person's life. If not interrupted, it causes death.

Spiritual Bankruptcy

All addictions affect our morality: They result in spiritual bankruptcy. On a daily basis, work addicts are dishonest, controlling, self-centered, perfectionistic, and abusive to themselves and others. No wonder their morality is affected. You cannot lead such a life without losing your moorings. Your grounding in basic values is lost in the relentless pursuit of the addiction.

Spiritual bankruptcy is the final symptom of workaholism; it usually heralds a dead end. It means you have nothing left. Many workaholics have said, "I no longer knew right from wrong in any of my dealings. And I despaired there was a God out there who could help me." I believe this aspect of workaholism is the most terrifying. It is frightening to be out of touch with a power greater than yourself and to find your disease, which you know is destructive, ruling you.

Fortunately, when the workaholic downward spiral is reversed, spirituality is one of the first things recovering people regain.

4. Workaholism's Deadly Continuum

One of the popular myths about workaholism and other addictions is that you have to "hit bottom" before you are motivated to begin recovery. This is not true. The sooner one can recognize the disease process and interrupt it, the better—although some workaholics must fall into the later stages to realize the severity of the addiction.

On page 48 is a continuum, or scale, for charting the progression of the disease of work addiction. It is similar to the widely used Jellnick Scale, which has traditionally been used in the diagnosis and treatment of alcoholism. The scale shows the early, middle, and late stages of the disease. Following the scale is a more detailed explanation of each step in the disease. In chapter 11, I complete the scale, showing the steps back up through recovery and healthy functioning. It is possible to use this chart as an early warning sign, and to begin taking steps to turn around these potentially fatal patterns.

In the early stages of the disease, many workaholics have symptoms they mistakenly believe to be temporary or situational symptoms of stress. Yet the more I learn about this disease, the more I realize that these are early warning signs of lifelong patterns.

In the early stages, workaholics often "do" life in a manner characterized by *rushing, busyness, overcaring, and rescuing others.* You can never get the attention of these workaholics because they are off on another mission. Children and loved ones complain, "You don't pay any attention to me." Along with

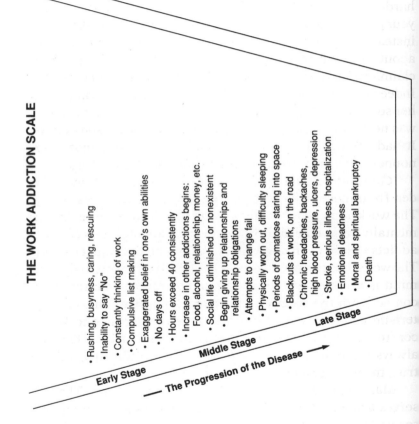

THE WORK ADDICTION SCALE

Early Stage
- Rushing, busyness, caring, rescuing
- Inability to say "No"
- Constantly thinking of work
- Compulsive list making
- Exaggerated belief in one's own abilities
- No days off
- Hours exceed 40 consistently

Middle Stage
- Increase in other addictions begins:
  Food, alcohol, relationship, money, etc.
- Social life diminished or nonexistent
- Begin giving up relationships and
  relationship obligations
- Attempts to change fail
- Physically worn out, difficulty sleeping
- Periods of comatose staring into space
- Blackouts at work, on the road

Late Stage
- Chronic headaches, backaches,
  high blood pressure, ulcers, depression
- Stroke, serious illness, hospitalization
- Emotional deadness
- Moral and spiritual bankruptcy
- Death

The Progression of the Disease →

this characteristic is the *inability to say "no."* Many work addicts take on more than they can handle. This trait arises out of codependency (saying "yes" when they mean "no" in order to please), and also out of an *exaggerated belief in their own abilities.*

Inevitably, work addicts are so task oriented, and outwardly oriented, that they rarely acknowledge their own personal limits. And they cope with life's problems by working harder, doing more. An overly busy housewife dealt with her young son's hospitalization by inventing more tasks to do instead of stopping and letting herself feel her panic and fear about him. When relatives offered to pitch in, she resisted, claiming that her rushing around kept her mind off her worry. Indeed it did; but it also prevented her from being available to her son, who needed her desperately. In addition, her rushing was not a new pattern developed just to meet her son's crisis. It had been going on for years and only became more pronounced as she avoided her feelings around his illness.

Constantly thinking of work is a characteristic that is hidden from most observers. In this, the work addict is tricky. The work addict can be playing volleyball, while in reality be mentally involved in a project at work. Some spouses of work addicts feel they can never reach the addict. This makes sense. The workaholic isn't "at home," he or she is gone mentally. The mind is a vehicle by which the addict can constantly make contact with the supply of the work addiction. This characteristic also serves the denial system of the workaholic. When confronted with excesses, the addict can claim, "I'm not always working, I spend time with you." Physically, this is true; mentally and emotionally, it is not.

Many work addicts are *compulsive list makers.* The list serves as a constant reminder of all that there is to do and seems to portend that one can never get caught up. Work addicts are not present mentally, and the list becomes essential as memory begins to fail. As their lives become more chaotic, the list is their only reference for what to do when. Internal priorities fall by the wayside; the list rules.

Workaholics have the feeling they will never catch up. Initially, they begin using weekends and evenings to get ahead of the demands they feel, whether those demands come from their environment or they create them out of their addiction. This occasional practice gradually becomes the usual pattern until they find that they have *no days off*. Compulsive rescuers fall into the same habits. A minister who was vacationing with his family found himself listening to people's problems and spending hours advising them. The purpose of his trip was to get away from exactly these behaviors and to spend time with loved ones.

Eventually, the work addict wakes up one day to find that the work week *consistently exceeds forty hours*. No longer the exception, the actual fact is that forty hours just do not do it anymore. Although forty hours is not a magic number, it is a generally accepted standard for those who have other aspects to their lives—family, physical and mental health, and social involvements. The hours issue for work addicts is that the addiction drives them to the extent that all limits are expendable. When workaholics stop monitoring their hours spent working, they are out of control of their lives and usually in the grip of the disease. They are leaving the early stages of work addiction and entering the middle stage of the disease.

In the middle stages of work addiction, work addicts begin to protect the disease and to lie about it. They have the definite sense that their lives have been taken over by something other than their own motivation, process, or goals. During this stage we frequently see an *increase in other addictions*. There may be excessive use of alcohol, spending may get out of hand, addictive relationships crop up. It is easy for loved ones to become confused at this stage of the disease. Whereas work is likely to be the primary addiction, the family wonders if the loved one is really an alcoholic or an overeater. The substance addictions are easier to detect. Often other addictions are simply backup or secondary addictions, which serve to take the edge off the pain and denial surrounding work addiction.

During the middle stage, *social life diminishes greatly* and the workaholic *begins giving up relationships and relationship obligations.* For one thing, there is no time for relationships. They would take the time and attention the addiction now uses. For another thing, the people close to the addict are the first ones to notice there is a problem. If the workaholic can be observed over time by those who know him or her, there is the likelihood that before long someone will be on to the disease. All addicts isolate. They believe they are unique—terminally unique, in some cases. Without the input of others, the workaholic can persist in the illusion that the disease is normal.

Most workaholics look very competent and in charge on the outside, while inside they are in chaos. They feel panic. At this stage in their workaholism they may feel *physically worn out* and *they are having difficulty sleeping.* They are running on hyped-up adrenaline, and coming down is difficult even though they feel physically exhausted. They may actually attempt to change, with the result that *attempts to change fail.* Usually the attempts are ineffective because they are temporary and do not recognize the disease concept of workaholism. They are based on good intentions and promises, which the workaholic has no hope of keeping. Also, attempts to change are rarely wholistic. They often address only one part of the disease.

In an effort to change his compulsive working, a computer programmer decided against bringing his laptop computer home. That change dealt with one aspect of his disease as it focuses on his computer. Next he sequestered himself in his tool shop with the same energy that had gone into his computer. Then he set aside time for his family every evening, but continued to think compulsively about his work. By now he was exhausting himself with attempts to change individual behaviors. What's more, most of his attempts were done in isolation, without first admitting he was powerless over his disease and then asking for help.

The later stages of the disease begin with the onset of serious physical and mental symptoms. At this point the workaholic fluctuates between periods of intense activity and *comatose staring into space.* This schizophrenic pattern contains *blackouts,* during which the work addict appears conscious but has no recall of certain activities. This is more severe than forgetting appointments or losing one's keys. The workaholic cannot account for various time periods. During these blackouts, workaholics may endanger their lives or the lives of others. Workaholics who handle toxic materials or who drive a lot are especially at danger during blackouts.

Throughout all stages of the disease, work addicts are experiencing mild physical ills. By the late stage, the symptoms are severe enough to impair the addict. The most common symptoms are *severe headaches, backaches, high blood pressure, ulcers, and depression.* These illnesses are chronic and they are now slowing down the workaholic. Perhaps physicians are sounding warnings about "cutting back" or "changing lifestyle." If these warnings are not heeded, the disease continues, and eventually a *stroke or serious illness* results in *hospitalization.*

By now the workaholic is feeling inextricably in the throes of the disease, both the physical debilitating disease and the addictive disease process. In addition, the person feels *emotionally dead and spiritually bankrupt.* It is as if all the reserves have been spent and there is nothing else to fall back on. This is the critical stage for the workaholic.

Hospitalization may provide enough of a scare to interrupt the pattern and provide enforced rest, but late-stage work addicts often continue working from their hospital beds. For them, it is usually only a matter of time before workaholism runs its inevitable course and ends in *death.*

5. Women & Workaholism

I am uncomfortable with self-help books. As I prepared to write this section of *Working Ourselves to Death*, I perused several excellent books on women's burnout, perfectionism, and self-esteem issues. I did so with a gnawing sense of dis-ease. All of the authors describe women's symptoms, and then offer tools and techniques for healing. What was missing was any reference to the role of the society, except as background. I am increasingly uneasy with our tacit acceptance of our organizations' and our society's right to work us to death.

Clearly, workaholism is an individual's disease. We're all becoming more knowledgeable about addictions in ourselves and in our families. However, to keep our focus pointed solely at the individual and not turn a laser light at the society is blindness approaching stupidity. Addictions are individual, family, institutional, and societal diseases. Nowhere is this truth so self-evident as in the case of women and work addiction.

Before examining the dimensions of women's workaholism, let us look at the social context within which they live and work. An old saying goes, "A man works from dawn to setting sun, but a woman's work is never done." The statistics seems to bear out the truth of these words. Sixty percent of all women in the United States work or are looking for work. This is 20 percent more than in 1970. Today, less than 10 percent of all households are composed of a working husband and a full-time homemaker wife; and in 57 percent of all families both parents are working full-time to make ends meet.

Thirty-eight percent of all children will spend time in single-parent households, and one out of every two marriages ends in divorce. Single-parent families in which mothers are the sole earners are on the rise. Across the board, a divorced woman's standard of living decreases by 73 percent, while a man's increases by 42 percent in the first year of divorce. Add to this figure the fact that, beginning in 1973, real wages began to fall, and had declined 13.8 percent by 1986. It is no surprise, then, that leisure time has shrunk by 37 percent since 1973, and for the first time in this century the work week is lengthening rather than decreasing.

Consistently, women earn less than men in almost all fields except a few, and those exceptions are so rare as to make no dint in the overall profile. Given the fact that women make less money, have fewer opportunities for advancement, cluster in dead-end jobs, and raise children singlehandedly in the majority of divorced families, is it any wonder that they are prime candidates for work addiction?

We all need to take responsibility for our health and wellness, and we need to address societal addictive processes as well. A mother who worked in a factory, cleaned office buildings at night, and delivered pizzas on weekends said, "Maybe I am one of those workaholics. I don't quite know for sure. I do know I'm so tired I could cry from the weariness and I do know I got three kids to feed and clothe. That's all I have time to know." When your very life depends upon working, like this mother, you may be a reluctant workaholic trying to survive in an addictive, nonfunctional society.

Erica's Story

Erica "woke up" the day she passed out! The day after she resigned from a particularly stressful job, she collapsed— unconscious—in a restaurant. She had no pulse, and for a few minutes she appeared dead. When she regained consciousness she said she knew her life was at stake. She had to make some changes.

Work addiction was a generational disease in Erica's family of origin. "My family did things, we didn't feel things." And the doing was seductive because it was so creative. Erica's family did unusual things, like taking three-week burro trips and making skis out of barrel staves. Her mother's world was a world of projects, and one project followed another. Most of the projects were fun, and from this Erica developed a horror of things she could not turn into fun. In addition, she believed she was what she did. She hadn't learned she was lovable for herself. "I never had frozen feelings," she quipped, "they were never born." Erica recalls a good friend asking her how she felt, and Erica thought that meant "did I have a pain in my knee or a headache. It never occurred to me that she was asking how do I feel about an idea, or just plain how do I feel."

Erica became an elementary school teacher—a perfect environment for her playfulness and her workaholism. She taught all day and did extracurricular activities in her spare time. Meanwhile, she had three small children and divorced her husband when her youngest was four. After six years of teaching a different grade in a different building, Erica changed jobs. Besides, she was struggling to support her children and herself on her teacher's salary, and it was proving to be inadequate.

Erica took a job as a financial consultant. Suddenly, she found herself in an environment that made the school system look like a picnic. To be successful as a financial consultant, she had to work seventy hours a week and study for licensing exams. In all, she was putting in ninty hours a week as well as being a perfect mother, baking, taking kids to appointments, and so on.

In her first year in the field, Erica made more money than she had teaching and she was the top earner in the company. Her earnings were adequate for the family's needs, so she told her manager she didn't need more money. She preferred time at home. Her manager came back with the requirement that she increase her production by 25 percent. Erica said good-bye to this company after accumulating client names and job hunting on the sly. "Ours was not a corporate environment in which you could be open about what you were doing." Erica was having lunch with friends the day she left the financial consulting company, and it was during lunch that she passed out.

In retrospect, Erica sees that her body was giving her warning signs. Physically, Erica felt "drugged" even though she wasn't using any medication. She had bouts of serious illness, but she would not go to bed. At one point she was so anemic she required a massive blood transfusion. Her blood count was so low no one could believe she could be out of bed. She frequently got strep infections that developed into the acute stage before she was aware of how sick she was.

Next, she was compulsively concerned that her three children be perfect in every way. She had isolated herself so that there was only work and family. Any leftover energy went to the children, and it was all spent on being sure they would be perfect. "I see now that I was using my children. If they were perfect, I could persist in the illusion I was OK. I didn't have to look at myself and what I was doing to my life."

Erica's denial was in direct proportion to the pain she was avoiding. After she named her work addiction and began her recovery from it, she got in touch with some early incest memories. She feels that her ready acceptance of workaholism blocked the pain and memories of the incest. Although dealing with the incest has not been easy, Erica feels relief at finally understanding her family story. She is no longer using work to prevent her from feeling, and thus she moves toward healing.

An interesting footnote to Erica's story concerns her new business venture. Erica decided she could not continue financial consulting in a corporate environment. Her recovery from her work addiction was too fragile for her to get back in the rat race, so she went into business with two other financial planners. Actually, the three share office space and work independently of one another. Erica insisted upon this arrangement, for she knew she would require more free time than the others and she did not want to be in an environment that had expectations of overtime.

Even though Erica's coworkers have no financial ties to her, they look disapproving when she leaves at 5 P.M. or takes time off for travel. She hears snide remarks about her "lazy" lifestyle or, "I wish I could live as freewheeling as you do," from people whose lives are dominated by workaholism. These people feel uneasy in the presence of Erica, who is doing something about her addiction. Erica's healing is a threat to her partners' disease, and they subtly put her down rather than face their own issues about work.

Erica's story is the prototypical story of women work addicts: the denial of feelings early in life; the tendency to choose a women's profession (teaching, nursing, secretarial), where demands are great and salary and advancement are poor; the refusal to pay attention to physical symptoms; the projection of perfectionistic expectations onto children; and the upping of stressors in her life, while at the same time becoming less capable of judging the effects. Notice that nowhere in Erica's story is there the assumption that she lacks the ability to do what she wishes to do. She moves smoothly from teaching to financial consulting.

For women and for women workaholics, the issue is not ability. Women tend to be realistic about ability. The issue is belief in themselves. "At some deep level," Erica reports, "I felt inadequate. I simply wasn't good enough." Workaholism worms its way right into that place in us where we feel we aren't good enough. It tries to fill a void externally through relentless busyness.

In 1981 Anne Wilson Schaef identified the void or emptiness women feel as the "original sin of being born female."[1]
She saw the void as a feeling we carried about our inadequacy
based on being women in a predominantly white male society.
Like the original sin concept, we were born with it, and no
amount of action by us or others could fill the void. We felt
ourselves innately inferior.

A friend once observed that "work is the addiction of
choice of the unworthy." Colette Dowling makes a similar
point in her book *Perfect Women*. She describes how women's
hidden fears of inadequacy actually drive us to perform. Our
sense of self is not separate from our achievements; rather it
actually depends upon achievements:

> Much of our frantic activity is symptomatic, an attempt to sup-
> press or deny low self-esteem. Woman's sense of Self has not
> always developed along with her achievements. In fact, sense of
> Self too often *depends* upon achievement. This, as we shall see,
> is what accounts for the driven-ness so many of us feel.[2]

Dowling and others point out that our frantic activity is
an attempt to attain an identity through doing. And more than
just doing: doing well, doing perfectly, and doing in such a
way that we please others. All of this striving gets us nowhere
internally, for working, caring, and pleasing do not resolve
the issue of low self-esteem.

Ellen Sue Stern, the author of *The Indispensable Woman*,
sees that the self-esteem issue for women manifests itself in
our trying to become indispensable. Historically, women's
role has been that of nurturer, so that self-esteem derived
from our ability to relate and to anticipate other's needs.
Becoming indispensable goes way beyond nurturing. Stern
believes that

> Our unconscious goal is to be so desirable, so smart, so compe-
> tent, so giving, so perfect, that others will be convinced they
> can't get along as well, if at all, without us. In our efforts to guar-

antee career security and advancement, to hold on to our relationships, and, mostly, to create and maintain a positive image of ourselves, we pretend we are infallible and that nothing is beyond our scope.[3]

The fact is that today's women are overworked simply by the societal demands of both wage work and housework. A recent tabulation of a working woman's week included 25 items. Among them: work, commute time, returning calls, time with kids, grocery shopping, cooking, housekeeping, pet care, visiting parents/relatives, laundry, repairs, reading. These and other activities amounted to 168 hours of potential work, which is 24 hours a day, 7 days a week. This is pressure enough.

The work addict compounds this pressure by making herself indispensable. She works harder and may even bemoan the pressure. But the fact is, she is reluctant to let the pressure go because being indispensable reassures her that she is valued and needed.

Becoming indispensable to others has long been recognized as one of the chief characteristics of the codependent, the person who dysfunctionally supports an active addict in his or her addiction. A tendency of many codependents is to look outside themselves for clues about how to act, what to feel. This external referenting is often characteristic of women workaholics. Many women work addicts report that they found their workaholism arising out of their codependency. It may have taken the form of excessive pleasing and then moved on to busyness, rushing, caring—all components of workaholism.

Other workaholic women have close ties between their relationship addictions and their workaholism. An executive secretary told me she was so intent upon pleasing her male boss, whom she idealized, that she never complained about working overtime and even demurred when he offered her time off. She believed her dedicated working bought his admiration; her loyalty bought his friendship. Her own process and needs were not considered.

The boss, himself a workaholic, loved her hard work (not her) and piled work on her. He became less enthusiastic when she began making errors and getting physically sick. When she finally left the job exhausted, she became almost suicidal with the realization that she was an object to this man, discarded when no longer useful. Doubly sickening was her realization that she had let herself be used in this way, that she had devoted countless hours of loyal effort in exchange for one ten-second pat on the head. In the end it was hollow. She felt empty and done-in by her illusion of a relationship, and equally done-in by the constant effort that it brought.

Other women workaholics report nearly chronic bladder infections. They refuse to take time to go to the bathroom especially when they work around men. They describe snickers and eye rolling during meetings when they excuse themselves. Externally referenting themselves to the approval of men, these women would actually hold their urine for up to ten hours. Several women reported that they had to urinate so badly that they could not make it into their homes upon return from work and would pee in the bushes outside their houses.

When I heard their story, I felt it was an extreme example of self-abuse arising out of codependence (worrying about what men think) and workaholism. The story was related to me in a large gathering of women. To my surprise, many heads nodded and all around me women began telling similar stories or saying that they had friends who had done the same. The need to win men's approval, coupled with progressive disengagement from awareness of their own physical needs, was resulting in illness of women on a wider scale than I had imagined. Workaholism and relationship addiction is a combination dangerous to one's health.

Not all women work addicts work. Some have well-organized home lives and work lives that are predictable and limited. Their addiction is to unceasing concern, caring, thinking, and figuring out things. Outwardly, they appear calm; inwardly, they are a bundle of furious mental activity, much of it superficial.

I knew a woman who could spend hours "making arrangements." If you needed directions, she provided you with three or four alternative routes, none of them simple. Or the children had to get to appointments and her husband to the airport. She would launch out on a plan followed by, "But what if this . . . ? And how will we that?" She had a gift for complicating the simplest arrangements. Of course all the codependents around her always allowed themselves to be sucked into working on the arrangements as well, until everybody's eyeballs were rolling with the unforseen complexity. The family would go away from these interactions confused and irritable, with the sense that their mother was incapable of creating or accepting a simple plan.

Workaholism prevents intimacy with ourselves and with others. The compulsive arranger had contact with her loved ones over issues that appeared significant for their lives together, but the process prevented intimacy. The end result was that people fled the mother and avoided such interactions. She felt misunderstood and unappreciated and played the martyr, believing she had the entire weight of making arrangements. Perhaps without her compulsive activity the family would have had other issues to discuss, issues too threatening to bring up; or perhaps this mother may have felt worthless without her role as arranger.

Women do not have to be in the corporate world to approach life like workaholics. Whenever we substitute our busyness and rushing and compulsiveness for doing our own inner process, we are on the way to work addiction and probably to burnout as well.

In the past, some writers had felt that workaholism was primarily a male addiction. Such images as the "man in the

gray flannel suit," the "company man," and men as "breadwin-
ners" fed this myth. In today's society, it is simply not true that
workaholism is the prerogative of men. As women enter into
parity with men in the job market, they also begin showing
evidence of characteristically male diseases. Heart disease is
on the rise in women, as is alcoholism. Work addiction is rampant among women.

Today, the societal demands on women to be competent in
multiple areas are coupled with nagging self-esteem issues
arising out of the need for women to prove they are worthwhile. This is a deadly combination. It leads so inevitably to a
setup for work addiction that one wonders why all women
aren't in this sinking ship.

6. Men & Workaholism

Workaholism, like the other addictions, is no respecter of gender. It affects men and women equally. Yet, as I set out to do this book, I questioned whether men and women experienced their workaholism differently. My interviews and experience showed me that the disease cuts a wide highway of symptoms we all drive down, regardless of gender. At the same time there are characteristics that appear to be unique to men, just as there are characteristics unique to women.

As we saw in the previous chapter on women and work addiction, there is a social context for women's workaholism. There is a social context for men as well. Whereas women are born feeling innately inferior due to the "original sin" of being born female, men suffer from the opposite myth. They arrive with the onerous burden of being born innately superior. They are born and socialized into what Schaef calls the myths of the white male system: They are innately superior, they know and understand everything, it is possible to be logical and rational at all times, their reality is the only reality that exists, and it is possible to be God as understood by the white male system.[1]

Women work themselves to death to fill the void of inadequacy. Men work themselves to death to live up to the legacy of these myths that are theirs alone.

Each of these myths requires workaholism to support it, and believing these myths leads men out of themselves and into addiction. Women say, "I'm not enough, therefore I must *do* to prove I am." Men say, "I must preserve my inheritance of superiority by doing these things. It is what is expected."

The societal myths men live by lead into tremendous needs for control and perfection. Jake, a social service worker in an agency for delinquent children, said that he found himself immersed in work addiction because he believed he should be a model for the other workers. He was a supervisor, and he felt that he should set a good example and be perfect in every way. He bought into the myth of innate superiority in two ways: as a man and as a manager. He attempted to control himself in such a way that he would be above criticism. His perfectionism extended to activities visible and invisible to others. He became so perfectionistic about the appearance of his letters that he would redo them several times until they were above reproach.

For Jake the issue wasn't low self-esteem, it was living up to expectations he accepted about being a manager. This acceptance fed into compulsive control and constant working, because the standards for "superior" were frequently unattainable.

Another man, Don, is a prime example of the effect of living out of the myths that it is possible to know and understand everything and it is possible to be entirely logical and rational. Don's workaholism does not keep him working excessive hours, but his *way* of working is entirely compulsive.

Don works for the Department of Natural Resources as a water quality engineer. His job entails doing studies on the environmental impact of pollution on fish and wildlife. Sixty percent of Don's work is with a team of other engineers. Using scientific studies, the team recommends policy to the department. Unfortunately, science is not all that exact a discipline. For example, studies show that when certain chemicals are placed in a stream, the fish will die. They put the chemicals in the stream, the fish don't die, and Don's department doesn't know why. These sorts of occurrences drive Don wild because (1) science is supposed to be exact, and (2) there should be an answer to everything.

Don is constantly thinking about these puzzles, and he has a gift for making the simple complex. His mind works overtime. To achieve certainty, he instructs his staff to repeat studies over and over. Don believes there is an answer "out there" and he should find it. In the end, it will be right and he will be right. Unfortunately, his efforts prove successful about 50 percent of the time, giving him enough reenforcement to believe his excessive thinking pays off.

Don is extremely difficult to work around; he is worse at home. He is tyrannical with his children. He needs to know everything they do. "Where'd you go?" "Out." "What'd you do?" "Nothing," is not acceptable to him. He insists his children have answers and reasons for everything they do and it all must make sense.

To protect themselves, Don's family avoids him, withholds information that can lead to an interrogation, or makes up answers they know will satisfy him.

Don is terrified of experiencing his uncertainty. Without the myth that it is possible to know and understand everything, he would be like everyone else—human, not innately superior.

I have encountered very few men whose identity was not bound up with the social pressure to be a "breadwinner." Even junior high school boys tell me they need a good job as adults to support a family. Few men feel they have a real option to not work. Their very identity as men is tied to work, often not just for their own livelihood, but to support others.

Schaef has observed that women in our society are perceived as sex objects by men, while men are perceived as marriage objects by women. "Get one" and you'll have financial and emotional security for life. Although this attitude is clearly a myth, it dies slowly.

Recently, a young man shared that he was considering marrying a woman he had been seeing. He added that his money would be tight, because he would be taking on the responsibility of paying his new wife's school loan after their marriage. When I questioned him on this (the woman was employed and it was her loan, after all), he said he felt the loan was a burden, but he believed as a husband it was his obligation. So he would take on the debt even though his future wife was capable of repayment.

I believe this kind of thinking is very prevalent among both men and women. With these benefits, what woman wouldn't want a husband?

Even before the marriage, this young man is already feeling a burden not of his own making, but taken on willingly. He will do this throughout his life, as do the majority of men, all in the service of an innate belief in what constitutes maleness and superiority. This type of conditioning is what men have learned from childhood. It is being "a good boy."

Women are not the only ones who set aside their personal needs to serve others. Boys learn this self-sacrifice as well, as Al's story exemplifies.

"All my life I heard, 'Be a good boy,'" said Al. "And I looked around and saw that a 'good boy' doesn't complain, he doesn't cry, he does the right thing, he makes his parents proud, and he follows the rules."

So Al was a good boy. He married, had a large family, worked as a translator in a publishing company. He thought that the right thing was working hard to support his family. When Al's wife began an affair with a friend, he tried to be understanding. His rule of not crying had resulted in progressive alienation from his own feelings, so Al tried to be reasonable. "Reasonable" eventually resulted in depression. Because Al had spent so many years living by the external rules of the good boy, he had no experience of his own needs. As his marriage became rockier, he began to work harder at his job. It was the one thing he knew well, and it dulled the terror that something awful was happening in his family. Al was learning that playing by the rules and being a good boy did not necessarily bring happiness.

Through a recovery group, Al began to see that his good boy message, supported by his excessive working, had resulted in his being totally out of touch with his own needs. He systematically cut back on work and took alone time to see if he could get even a glimmer of his feelings. Slowly, Al got in touch with the pain he felt for all the ways he had ignored his own process and lived out his parent's rules. Because Al had this realization in his sixties, he felt he had many lost years to grieve.

As Al worked less and lived out of his own process instead of his myths, his wife found him a more interesting person to be around. She had complained bitterly that he was not available to her either physically or emotionally. Her complaint was valid. Al's work addiction took him away from all personal relationships; his "good boy" myth was a mask. Al's wife didn't have a real person with whom she could relate.

Women overwork to please others and meet their needs; men overwork to meet external expectations. Both become unavailable to themselves and to loved ones.

The last myth of the white male system is, "It is possible to be a god, as understood by the system." This is the god of the *omnis*—all-present, all-powerful, all-perfect, all-seeing, all-controlling. I think this myth has been very prevalent in men's workaholism. It is especially seen in those men who choose "godlike" professions such as medicine, law, the ministry, or any profession where others entrust their lives to them. Whenever men see themselves as solely responsible, they are operating out of the god illusion. Frequently, workaholics push their bodies with such intensity that they give out. This is often a surprise to the god-illusion work addict.

God-illusion work addicts often swing between a dualism: They see themselves as God or as bag ladies. They have a terrible fear that if they let up for a moment, dire poverty is around the corner.

Bill was the physician who couldn't heal himself. His codependence and his workaholism were hooked early in his training by the explicit messages he received. He felt himself responsible for his patients' healing, and his residency established the pattern of eighty- and ninety-hour work weeks—a common practice in medicine.

Since Bill was to be all things to all people, he began taking responsibility for every aspect of his practice. Although he loved medicine, he found himself spending more and more hours on the administration of his office, bookkeeping, legal issues, and even ordering supplies. Bill's intelligence and quick mind proved a hindrance, because he could do every job in the clinic better than his own staff. Consequently, when they would make mistakes, Bill would cover for them. Then he would feel angry and resentful that they were letting him down. He said that he longed to have his staff take responsibility, and he believed that he delegated. In reality, however, his staff felt watched and was terrified of making errors. Their tension caused them to make more errors than if they had been relaxed, and the situation in the clinic eroded from bad to worse. Staff could not set boundaries with Bill. If he worked from 7 A.M. to 7 P.M., he expected the same of them. As Bill's work addiction spilled over into their lives, staff began resigning for self-preservation.

Bill was bitterly disappointed with the lack of dedication of his staff, and his perfectionism was such that he measured the success of the day by whether anyone had "messed up." If one mistake had been made, he focused on that and personalized the mistake as if it were a personal assault on him and his reputation as a physician. His glass was always half-empty.

Bill's wife and several colleagues expressed concern. They were fearful for his well-being and also for his patients.

Patient care was the one place where Bill had near total control. So far, that had not been affected, but friends were worried it was next. Unfortunately, Bill's superior intelligence was his greatest obstacle. He was astute and gifted in so many ways that if things fell apart around him, he simply worked harder. Gods do it all themselves; humans ask for help.

Bill's illusion of godliness came to a screeching halt the day he suffered a massive coronary. He was forty-one years old, and had been working 110 hours a week for three years straight. His recuperation lasted three months. His staff sought other jobs, and patients sought other physicians. The very qualities that had helped Bill survive medical school — his intelligence and ability to work long hours — were killing him now.

It is important to see in Bill's story the collusion of the medical profession in his addiction. Medicine prepared him to be godlike by building inhuman expectations into the training program of physicians. Moreover, as Bill began his physical recovery and his addiction recovery, he found very little understanding among other physicians. They looked upon him as a poor bloke who just couldn't take the heat of the profession.

Medicine has been slow to admit the fact that there are many (estimated at one in eight in a 1989 survey) active addict MDs. The greatest concern has been around the physically impaired physician using drugs and alcohol. "A workaholic?" laughed a physician I consulted. "Why the whole profession is workaholic. How can that be a disease?"

I am pessimistic that professions like medicine will willingly recognize the destructiveness of workaholism. To do so would appear to undermine the very premises on which the field is based — the white male god-illusion myth.

The men in my life and in my consulting practice have taught me a lot about workaholism. I always felt, from my own experience and that of other women, that women are born feeling second class. We believe we can't have it all because we aren't whole. Therefore we frequently seek relationships and jobs with the hope they will make us whole. This attitude is a trap, and usually leads to addiction—either addictive relationships, overeating, or working ourselves into numbness.

Men, on the other hand, carry the weight of trying to live out the myths of the white male system. They find themselves little gods from birth, and are constantly trying to live up to an impossible birthright. The mismatch between what society says they are supposed to be and how they really experience themselves is a burden and a strain. Those who face into the discrepancy rediscover themselves and some balance in life. Those who don't drown their sorrow in addictive processes, workaholism being just one of the more acceptable forms in the white male system.

I have often wondered what our society would be like if men refused the myth of their innate superiority and recovered from their workaholism. I believe our society could not continue in its competitiveness and control were this to happen. Moreover, men would discover their true birthright: to be fully human and fully at home in this world as they are.

7. The Family & Workaholism

Addictions treatment took a leap forward the day it shifted its focus away from the individual addict and onto the addict in a system—the family. This was a radical shift, because it moved the field away from an individual disease concept to a systems view: The addict received help, and the family that was in deep trouble also got attention.

Early in the shift, it was thought that involvement by family members was a support to the recovering addict. In this view, the addict was still the problem and the family was the victim. Eventually, it became apparent that the family members were themselves addicts, or codependents. They had their own disease; an addictive process disease to be sure, but separate from the disease of the addict. When family members began focusing on themselves and their recovery instead of the addict in their lives, they also began healing.

Work addiction is a disease fraught with pitfalls for the family. It is, first of all, a confusing addiction. The typical addict is using drugs or alcohol, and family members see living proof that their loved one is in trouble. They feel embarrassed by activities of a drunk parent. Children and spouse generally develop a thick wall of denial around the addict, but the denial itself is in response to events they feel are wrong.

The workaholic's family frequently feels crazy. In the early stages of the disease, it is nearly impossible to identify the problem. In addition, unlike drugs and alcohol, the society is actively promoting work addiction. The family is probably surrounded by other families who are just like them.

"What's normal?" they wonder, and then back away from their perception that a loved one is in trouble. Nevertheless, the families of work addicts suffer greatly. They need help just as the workaholic does.

In this section we'll focus on the family in two ways. First, we'll describe the work addict in the family setting and identify the effects of the addiction on the family. Second, we'll look at the family as addicts with the workaholic.

The Work Addict in the Family

Work addicts have trouble restricting their disease to the job. After all, they are work addicts, not job addicts. Therefore the addiction does not stop at the front door of the house or the apartment. It comes with you wherever you go.

The workaholic lacks appropriate boundaries. Thus the workaholic process pervades everything. There is no difference between the workplace and the home. Workaholics take work to bed, take it home on weekends, and take it on vacation. The workaholic is never without work, because work is the fix.

Vacations are stressful for the families of workaholics. First of all, it is difficult to get addicts to agree to a vacation ahead of time, because they never know what might be happening at work six months hence. Then, if work addicts do agree to vacations, they may be totally unavailable emotionally because they take work with them. Many children of workaholics describe vacations as whirlwinds of activity. Their parents do vacations the way they do work.

One boy told me of a trip to Hawaii in which his father woke him up at the crack of dawn to run on the beach. Then it was breakfast on the deck. Next a boat cruise around the coast. Lunch was on the run; hit the beach when the surf is up; dash back to the rental shack with the surfboards, gulp an island snack on the way back to the hotel, shower, drive madly to the end of the road to watch the sun go down over the ocean, meet friends for dinner, drop exhausted into bed.

Every day of vacation was similar until the boy pleaded, then demanded a day off to do what he wished to do. He wanted to lay around and read and watch videos and maybe hang out around town. His father, who saw the vacation as a chance to spend "quality time" with his son, grumbled and paced the hotel room. Finally, after mild threats to his son that he would be missing some fun, the father took off to see a waterfall.

The boy was racked with guilt over the vacation. He missed contact with his father and longed for time with him. He felt confused and conflicted. He was doing wonderful things, and he was spending more time with his father than he ever dreamed possible. Yet, by the end of the trip, he felt further removed from his father than before the vacation.

The boy's father was not present emotionally. He had not brought work along on the trip, he just transferred his workaholic pace to the leisure activities. The boy was as isolated as if the father had dropped him in the hotel and left; only it felt more confusing, because there was a body there but no person to relate to.

Workaholics are simply not available to their loved ones. Their disease tends to make them self-centered, but the disease is tricky enough that work addicts go through the motions of relating. If family members are at all aware, they know the relationship is superficial at best, nonexistent at worse.

Still, not all workaholics are totally removed from loved ones. When work addicts are present, they can be intensely present. They can be great lovers when they are aware. It is the inconsistency that is maddening. The workaholic does come home on time occasionally, so the family never knows if this is going to be one of those times. When confronted, the addict always has those times to use in defense of the denial about the addiction.

I believe that the lack of a significant emotional connection is the most devastating aspect of this disease for families. Workaholic families resemble families that have suffered the death of a loved one. You can see them going through the stages of denial ("This isn't happening to us"); bargaining ("If I do this, will you spend time with me?"); anger ("I'm furious that you've left me"); resignation ("This is just the way he is. I may as well get used to it"). The only problem is that the loved one is still walking around, a constant reminder of what could have been.

Work addicts have hobbies, but rarely are the hobbies a source of playfulness. Hobbies are turned into money-making ventures. Hobbies generate anxiety, deadlines, and more work. A young man told me about his father, who was a physician in the northwest and became interested in smoking salmon. He was handy with his hands, so first he built a smoking shed. Then he recruited the children to help fish for salmon. Since the shed was quite large, he decided to smoke enough fish to give to neighbors as gifts. This project then turned into a roadside stand with demands for more fish, more time in the smoking shed, and more of the family's time to take their turn working.

"The odd thing about it," said the young man, "was that we didn't need the money. My father made enough as a doctor. My family didn't like salmon that much. This was just a lark of my father's that we all got trapped in."

The father was rarely available to his family due to his medical practice. Now any free time was spent with the salmon venture. It became a source of anger and resentment for the family and a way to keep the father busy every "free" minute.

Sometimes workaholics become irritated with family members who have priorities other than work. Workaholic parents can set a tone in families in which incessant busyness is rewarded; staring into space, dreaming, and playing around aren't. Almost all adult children who are second-generation work addicts either learned their workaholism in the family or come from families where other addictions were present. The clue to these families is that busyness and work become a substitute for feeling.

A story of generational work addiction was shared with me by Amy, a woman who was on a fast track all her life. Her grandfathers were adventurers and frontier entrepreneurs. Her father was never at home nor at the births of any of his children. He wasn't capable of waiting. Amy discounted her mother, because Amy got all her strokes from her father for doing. She played tennis, skied, sang for the church, volunteered, and worked a regular job.

All of Amy's life decisions were dictated by work. She moved to cities she hated, because of work. She never considered staying in a locale she liked. She looked for social connections in work-related groups. She did not have a separate social life. During a depression over her inability to form close relationships with men, she confided her sadness to a colleague. He shot back, "How are you going to meet anyone but the janitor?"

Amy continued working. She joined a large company, optimistic that she could reorder her life; but really her world was collapsing. To meet the objectives her boss set took eighty hours a week. He asked her to sign a sheet of objectives specifying that she would do the work, and she knew she was done for. "I had no support system. No caring person to fall back on. I had worked myself to a skeleton and there was no flesh left. I was out of reserves. The corporate values were things I didn't believe in. Inside I was emotionally bankrupt. I couldn't be who they wanted me to be."

Amy dropped out of work completely, left all civic involvement, and took time to discover who she was and what she wanted to do with her life. During this time her generational connection with her workaholic father became painfully clear. Her father was the one person to whom she related, because they talked about work. Now she was trying to drop work—her only tangible connection with him. When she met with him to share developments in her life, he was silent. He had nothing he could ask her now that she wasn't working. When Amy queried her father about this, his only reply was: "Well, what else is there?"

Amy has many memories of her father, but the one she cherishes most is the time they were on a deserted road and the car broke down. Far from help, they had to wait several hours for a tow truck. "It was the best time," she said. "He was always fixing and doing and here we were with a forced wait. He did something he never did before or since: He sat in the front seat, he gazed out the car window, he looked at me, and we just talked."

Listen to the themes in these stories. They are all the same, and the desires are so simple. Children just want a little time with parents. They want to *be with* someone they love and trust. They don't necessarily want anything from the parents. They don't seem to need activities, they just need to be with. But being with is impossible for work addicts, because they aren't capable of being with themselves, much less someone else. Even when they are trying hard, they can only do what they know best, their addiction.

Undeniably, work addiction is destroying families. Children and spouses are resigning themselves to making appointments to spend time with the workaholic. We now have the prevalence of "quality time," which in the addictive system is an excuse for too little time or preoccupied time. *Time* magazine ran a cover article on how America is running itself ragged. Their conclusions? "Kids understand that they are being cheated out of childhood. Eight-year-olds are taking care of three-year-olds. There is a sense that adults don't care about them."[1] Increasingly, children are scheduled into multiple activities and pushed by their parents in order that the parents may protect their own work addiction. The result is a generation of workaholic kids.

The workaholic's disease pervades every corner of a family's life. It affects mealtimes, vacations, holidays, and every day. Children and loved ones feel conflicted, confused, and angry. As the work addict progresses in the disease, the family may shrug and do what they can to protect themselves. They may become workaholic themselves, or they may give up altogether.

The Family in the Addictive Process

The work addict exists in a system. When that system is the family, the family members, by definition, become enmeshed with the work addict's dysfunctional world unless they are actively recovering from it themselves. In a real way, the workaholic's dysfunctional system stays in place because members support it. Their support can be in the form of their denial about how crazy their parent or spouse is becoming. It can be based on their dishonesty about the effects of workaholism on them. Or they can spend time focusing on the workaholic, blaming the addict instead of dealing with their own needs.

Sometimes children are too young and helpless to assert their needs. In single-parent families, for example, eight-year-olds are hardly in a position to prevent a workaholic parent from affecting them. These youngsters develop survival-type behaviors of freezing their feelings, parenting siblings, and growing up fast. They become the next generation of adult children of addictive, dysfunctional families.

As seen in the earlier examples, workaholic parents raise children who cope by becoming workaholic children. Teachers and others who work with children have been increasingly alarmed at the frenetic, programmed activity they see among youngsters today. From day care through high school, children are pressured and pushed into the "right" schools, dancing lessons, language lessons, sports, computer camps, and myriad other activities. They are constantly occupied with doing. These children are not just living in a workaholic environment, they are child workaholics.

Another dysfunctional coping behavior is that of moving to the other end of the dualism. Instead of becoming workaholic themselves, some children and spouses stop altogether. They become paralyzed and incapable of any action.

Some families are aware of the work addicts' effect on them, yet feel very conflicted. Their conflict arises because the workaholic provides them luxuries they would not ordinarily have. This is a typical bind for upwardly mobile workaholic families.

In one such family, the father was the work addict. An insurance executive, he was able to provide more expensive things for his family year by year. They were living quite well—a large, new, custom-built home, a BMW, the latest high-tech equipment, and fabulous vacations in exotic spots around the world. The cost to him and to them? Ninety hours a week at work, extensive business travel, an exhausted father and spouse who was unavailable on the rare occasions when he was home.

I spoke with this man's wife. She told me her three teenagers were well aware of what was going on with him. They were angry and resentful about the loss of their father, and had urged their mother to do something. They suggested a family meeting with a facilitator to express their concern, or a session with a therapist—anything to stop the craziness in their household. This sounded good to me, so I asked the woman what she was going to do. She acknowledged that she was upset and worried about her husband's incessant working. Then she said, "I could not possibly confront him on this, after all he has done for me and the kids. He worked like a dog for us to support our standard of living. I would never criticize him or complain. It would only add to his burden. And it would be disloyal."

This woman was thoroughly enmeshed in her husband's workaholism. She "cared" for him by remaining silent about a disease process that would eventually kill him. Moreover, I believe her husband's addiction had benefitted her in a way that she was not willing to give up or at least change. This is the self-centeredness of the coaddict. Although it looks as if she is suffering or inconvenienced, she is not willing to unsettle herself enough to rock the boat of their arrangement. And although it may appear that confrontation will adversely affect the husband, in reality the wife is protecting herself.

The conflict experienced in the family, which is benefiting materially, goes in stages. Initially, there is excitement about acquiring sought-after material things. Next, there is conflict over the fact that the workaholic is inconsistently available and usually progressively absent. This stage is followed by resignation and an increase in spending as a justification for the neglect. "We deserve it," reasons the family.

Workaholics do adversely affect their families. Besides the damage done by lack of emotional closeness, the workaholic style creates little workaholics out of children. Families also participate in the addictive process by their silence and their resentment. Sometimes it is difficult to believe a loved one has a disease, for workaholics look good in the early stages. As the disease progresses, however, all family members become enmeshed. Consequently, recovery from workaholism becomes a family recovery as well as the workaholic's recovery.

8. The Work Addict on the Job

In *The Addictive Organization* Anne Wilson Schaef and I described the consequences of having active addicts in the workplace. Addicts practice their disease wherever they go. It cannot be put on hold in certain settings. It is the illusion of control to think it can. Many substance abusers try to limit their use to outside work hours. Of course they still are in their disease in their dishonesty, manipulation, moodiness, and self-righteousness, even though they appear dry on the job.

For the work addict, the job is like a chocolate factory for an overeater. It is as if an active alcoholic were going to work in a saloon. Whether your workaholism takes the form of work, rushing, busyness, or caring, the job is fertile soil. There are tasks galore, time limits, external measures, levels of accountability, and other people involved in the same process. What is more, you get paid for it. This is the addiction that is rewarded. There is an illusion that workaholics do not hurt anyone and they are good for the company. These ideas are not supported by the facts. Workaholics hurt themselves, others, and the company.

Workaholics share several characteristics in the work setting. They bring to work all of the characteristics described earlier as belonging to the individual workaholic. And, as workaholics, they have a unique way of doing their disease at work.

Obsessiveness is a primary characteristic on the job. Work addicts become obsessive about projects and tasks and they do not keep the whole picture before them. This is a very dysfunctional trait, especially for people whose work entails keeping many balls in the air. They often have the feeling they must drop everything and devote full attention to one issue. This can drive coworkers crazy, especially when they depend on the workaholic for certain information.

The other aspect of obsessiveness is focusing on the next project, thus removing attention and energy from the work at hand. Many workaholics do this. It's like anticipating your next drink or, in the case of the relationship addict, having a new relationship warming up as the present one deteriorates. The obsessor cannot live without something to do, so a constant flow of new things is necessary.

Like obsessors, some workaholics get hooked on innovation. Many companies that develop and patent new products report this problem. Their people become so hooked on the "new" and change, that they neglect follow-through or even adequate development. They cannot keep their attention focused long enough to finish what they have created. Moreover, they report boredom with follow-through. Upon deeper investigation, I discovered that these workers were hooked on the adrenaline rush of the new idea, and felt let down by the painstaking development work. They jumped to the new projects to get their high. Of course, with inadequate product development, these great innovations were just sitting on the shelves and not making any profit for the company.

Corporations today are desperate for innovations and creativity. Unfortunately, aside from the innovators described above, work addicts can offer little help in the area of creative new ideas. Workaholics have monotone minds. Their thinking becomes one-dimensional. Creative ideas often take time. They need the leisure of staring into space, play, some idle chatter. These processes are not tolerable for the workaholic.

Some professions are more prone than others to obsessive, getting-high activity. Men and women in the publishing industry get an adrenaline rush in at least two ways. One, the always have deadlines they are trying to meet to get new books out or articles ready. And, more seductively, their work is in the realm of new ideas, so there is always the excitement of being on the cutting edge.

Emergency room doctors and nurses say they live on a perpetual adrenaline high at work. They are in a constant state of readiness, expecting the next patient. An emergency room nurse left nursing because the pace interfered with her recovery from work addiction. She said she got such a high from her work that the rest of her life paled by comparison. Additionally, she felt that she left her self during the intense period of responding to constant crisis. She neglected the most basic self-care when she was on duty, resulting in fatigue, bladder infections, increased colds, and depression.

The healthy worker can be intensely involved in a project and then rest or ease off in slack time. Workaholics panic with slack time. Consequently, they tend to prolong tasks and make simple projects more complicated than they need be. Unconsciously, this prolongation keeps workaholics busy and effectively out of touch with themselves.

A manager complained that his team was always extending projects past deadlines. Upon closer scrutiny, it became obvious that one member of the team found something else that just had to be done before they could wrap up the design. Rather than confront this behavior, which was only one piece of an entire constellation of work addiction, the other team members tried to work around him or passively went along with him. This resulted in many missed deadlines, and incessant grumbling by the team. In addition, the company was losing money with every missed deadline.

It is important to appreciate the complexity of the work addict. In the previous example, the addiction manifests itself in slowing down projects that have deadlines. In the case of the innovators, the addiction manifests itself in rushing from one project to the next. In both cases, the workaholic doesn't do what is appropriate for the task. The self-centeredness of the disease is apparent. The task is irrelevant, even though work addicts appear to be unable to live without it. But, in truth, the actual work is not important; it is only a means to an end. The end is the high and/or the numbness, both of which take the workaholic out of touch with true awareness and feeling.

Workaholics love crisis and they precipitate crisis. Many workaholics were good crisis managers in their families of origin. They felt needed, and they were affirmed for bailing out other people. Also, crisis gives the addict, whose feelings may be shut down, a chance to feel. Crisis takes our attention away from the everydayness of our existence. It is another form of an adrenaline high.

I frequently counsel organizations: When you have constant crisis, look for an addict. You will usually have a workaholic at the center of it or resolving it.

Workaholics are usually not good team players for several reasons. One, workaholics need control; teams are cooperative efforts, so teams are a source of frustration for the work addict. Two, the best teams are composed of people who have a sense of self, think for themselves, and contribute their ideas into the pot with others. Workaholics fail on this score because they are out of touch with themselves, their thinking may be to please others, and their ideas are usually serving their addictive process rather than the needs of the team. Third, teams are groups that work together, not alone. Workaholics will isolate and work alone when others cannot be coerced into staying longer. This tendency is frustrating to workaholics. They will frequently work outside team time, come up with solutions they give to the team, and then look on bewildered when the team is angry about the violation of its process. In their tunnel vision and intensity, workaholic team members don't understand that it is not what they do but how they do it that is the problem.

Perfectionistic work addicts will spend countless hours preparing for the team meetings. They are terrified of failure, or fear that others will see them for who they really are. Of course, team membership is just an added burden for them.

Perfectionistic workers are inconsistent in terms of productivity. They fluctuate between intense working and procrastination. Consequently, they will work in spurts and then do nothing at all. One work addict observed, "I went between frantic activity and being almost paralyzed. My perfectionism was such that I was afraid to do anything lest it not be perfect, so I just became immobilized."

Again, it is important to notice the dualistic nature of the workaholic performance and to ask its effect on productivity. Intense, binge workers may be very productive, but they are "peaks-and-valleys" workers. When they are in a peak, their adrenaline is high and their hype looks good. But once they hit the high, they have no place to go but down. For good long-range productivity, they need to level out their performance.

Imagine the unpredictability peaks-and-valleys performers introduce into an organization. Since you never know when the addict will hit a high or a low, you are constantly steeling yourself for the next blow. I once had a secretary who suffered with this aspect of the disease. When she was "up" it was great for the office. Things fairly hummed along, although I must admit it felt manic at times. Inevitably, whenever I really needed her, she would hit a valley and I'd be without the support I thought I had hired in a secretary. I began to have a new appreciation for balance and the leveling out of performance. Such balance is extremely rare in a workaholic.

We have seen how workaholics use work as the ultimate excuse in their families and personal lives. "Don't count on it" is a phrase familiar to most workaholic families. It means never make plans because you never know when the addict will have to work, and work is the first priority. This is how work addicts avoid taking responsibility for their actions and decisions. There is a power greater than themselves driving them: their addiction.

The fact is, workaholics don't take responsibility on the job either. When they experience job dissatisfaction, they project blame on coworkers, managers, or the company. They do not examine their own lives and priorities. For the work addict, the buck stops out there, not with the self. By focusing externally, workaholics avoid facing the reality that they are destroying themselves. At the same time, they remain blind to the destructiveness to their home and organization.

A lot of workaholic employees want to "do it myself." They isolate for several reasons. In isolation they can keep control of the pace of work and of work itself. By isolating they do not have to ask for help. This supports the god illusion. Finally, the more isolated the employee, the more difficult he or she is to observe. It is unlikely you will intervene on a workaholic when you have no opportunity to observe his or her behavior. In all of these ways, work addicts protect their supply on the job.

Everything written here about workaholics and the job applies to managers as well as employees. In addition, there are a few other characteristics we see in managers. Workaholics are poor managers. Unfortunately, there are a lot of them in management positions today. This may be one reason there is so much management consulting going on. In business we all sense that something is wrong. We've neglected to see that the missing piece is that we've never addressed the addictive process in people and in organizations.

Sometimes, in an effort to do it right, managers give conflicting messages to employees. Cliff was such a manager. He managed a large social service agency. His employees worked odd hours, evenings, and weekends as they traveled to other cities giving workshops. Cliff, a nonrecovering workaholic, told his staff they should take at least one day a week for personal renewal and updating. They were, after all, expected to be up on the latest theories in the field.

Several employees took Cliff up on his recommendation. They announced that Wednesday would be their personal renewal day and they could be found at home reading. Although Cliff espoused the renewal in principle, he chaffed against it in practice. He never took a reading day for himself, and he frequently scheduled meetings for Wednesdays. When his staff reminded him that Wednesday was their day for personal renewal, Cliff would roll his eyes, sigh, and walk off in a huff. Soon it became increasingly difficult for the employees to maintain their day. Other employees groused about it, feeling inconvenienced, and so on. Cliff continued to give pep talks about taking time off, but everyone knew that it was an illusion and merely fed Cliff's belief that he was an enlightened and compassionate manager, when in fact he was in denial about his workaholism. His overt message and his actual behavior set up tremendous confusion among his staff. Eventually, new staff were oriented to the agency by old staff with the admonition: "Don't do what Cliff says, do what he does."

One of the reasons workaholic managers do poorly with employees is that they do not understand the concept of limits from their own experience. Their workaholism is rampant in their own lives. They are unable to tune into their own bodies and psyches. Because they can't monitor their own needs, they have no respect for others' needs. They have less understanding of employees' needs. They don't know what is realistic to expect and what is not. They are loose cannons in the organization. The problem is, they are in charge.

Everywhere I go I hear the same complaint: "My boss is a workaholic and expects the same from me." Workaholics are self-centered. They use themselves as the measure by which they judge others, so their norm for others is bound to be workaholism.

I saw this problem at the institutional level in a human services agency that hired me to mediate a conflict among its personnel. Upon investigation, it appeared that the workaholics were furious with other staff because they only worked forty hours a week and took vacations with their families. The workaholics were adamant that the other workers were not as dedicated as they were. They accused them of laziness and falling down on the job. In my sessions with staff, I found the forty-hour people to be hardworking. The difference between them and the others was that their job was not their life. This attitude infuriated the workaholics—the addiction seemed to have a bit of religious fervor—who felt their view of the world was the "right" one. The workaholics' norm created a split in the staff. It is a good example of how this disease process can be established and then become the expectation, when in reality it is dysfunctional and the people perpetuating it are sick.

Finally, we should not miss the fact that, as the disease of workaholism progresses, employees and managers make more mistakes, their judgment becomes impaired, and they burn out. As workaholism moves into a downward spiral, burnout makes the decision to quit inevitable. And of course, for the company, costs go up.

An extreme but not untypical example of this problem was a workaholic CEO who announced his resignation from his company on Wednesday. On Thursday, he suffered a slight stroke, which he refused to treat even though his family was frantic. On Friday, he gave his farewell speech to the employees from a wheelchair and was taken immediately to the hospital emergency room.

This story is the physical side of burnout. When the CEO quit, he fell apart. The irony of his story and many others like his is that, even in quitting, the pattern of his life remains the same. This man suffered from workaholism; as a result, he did not take care of himself during his working years. Now that he has had a stroke, he still doesn't take care of himself, his wife does. On one end of his life he was frantically active. Now he is immobile. In neither situation has he taken responsibility for his own process, his own care. This is the tragedy of physical burnout. Those who burn out emotionally at least have the chance that they can begin to heal and turn around the disease process.

9. The Workaholic Organization

It is painfully obvious that work addiction is a serious disease that affects individuals, their relationships, and their jobs. In all cases, it leads to physical and psychological impairment. In some cases it leads to death. Treatment professionals have become astute about how to intervene on this disease and treat it. We can even facilitate family recovery. But what do we do if the organization is the workaholic?

This question was posed to me by a woman who heads a wellness center on the campus of a very prestigious university. She joined one of the first Workaholics Anonymous groups in the United States because she found she was losing herself in her work. She has faithfully worked a program of recovery for her personal addiction and she is coming along well. The problem: Her job makes her crazy. With her fragile recovery, she walks into work only to meet rampant workaholism in the very fiber of her organization. She knows she is in a relationship with an addict, but in this case the addict is her organization. Her drive to fix it is high, which threatens her own sobriety.

Institutional workaholism? Her question was not a new thought, for earlier I had dealt with the fact that organizations in our society are operating exactly like an active addict.[1] Yet something in her question struck me, and I determined to look more closely at the ways in which organizations are more than a neutral setting for workaholic behavior.

Organizations are workaholic. They foster this disease, they promote it, and I believe they actually require it in order to survive. Consequently, organizations have a part in the illness and they have a responsibility for the recovery. They are neither victims nor innocent bystanders when it comes to workaholism.

Environment

Why are organizations workaholics? Let's look briefly at the environment within which our largest corporations are doing business today.

Following World War II, there were no major business competitors to vie with the United States. Both Germany and Japan were rebuilding devastated lands and economies. Economically, the United States was the world power. Now, with a massive deficit and formidable competition from around the globe, U.S. business is facing unprecedented losses.

Productivity and profitability are down. Since 1980, 2.8 million jobs have been eliminated at Fortune 500 companies, with 1 million of those from management. The U.S. workforce is characterized by indifference and poor quality. In 1987, American workers applied for more worker compensation than in any previous year.[2]

Real wages buy 13.8 percent less than they did in 1973, and people are working longer hours than ever before. For the first time in this century, young people cannot expect to be better off financially than their parents. The likelihood is that they will be worse off, with fewer able to buy a home and more of them returning to their parents' home to live.

A business associate put it this way: "When I graduated from college in 1952, I was in an economic climate in which I could expect to get a job with a good company, make a salary that would adequately support my family, and retire with security. I had evenings and weekends at home. It was rare to bring work home. My two sons scrambled to get their jobs. They know that if they let up, lined up behind them are a hundred well-qualified people waiting for their jobs. They leave home at 7 A.M. They rarely return home before 8 P.M. They always work at least one day on weekends and they bring work home every night. Their salaries are barely adequate and job security is nil. My thirty-two-year-old son developed a bleeding ulcer last year, my thirty-six-year-old son has blinding migraines."

This, then, is the climate in which organizations are attempting to do business and workers are attempting to survive. This environment is not an excuse for workaholism, and it does give us some clue as to why we may be seeing a rise in workaholism. It is important to remember, however, that work addiction is a progressive and fatal disease. Therefore it is the worst response to an already troubled economy. In no way can work addiction bale out a company. It can only bring the company down faster.

Corporate Survival Above All Else

Work addicts will do anything to maintain their fix or supply. Although they may feign concern for others, their actual goal is to protect the addiction. This results in massive self-centeredness. Organizations that are workaholic adapt a similar creed. They put their interests above everything else. They are answerable to no one—not workers, shareholders, communities, or the nation. When an organization is driven by self-interest, everyone is expendable and loyalties are not honored. This aspect of corporate workaholism may account for the rash of mergers, layoffs, and shutdowns. It also leads to the codependents (workers, shareholders, suppliers) scrambling to protect themselves from the destruction. Consequently, everyone is looking out for self and no one is putting energy into the organization.

Profitability At All Costs

The workaholic organization operates with tunnel vision. It sees one thing: the bottom line of the financial statement. To conserve profit, corners are cut with products and work is squeezed out of people. There is tremendous pressure on management to do more with less. Over the years, I have seen many organizations shift the weight of profitability directly onto people. Workers actually become commodities. They are used up and discarded and others wait in the wings to replace them.

To the extent that employees are codependent with the organization and fearful for their own survival, they cooperate with this madness. Employees, like children of a workaholic parent, develop coping strategies that are usually dysfunctional for them. They please the parent organization, try to anticipate its next move, they create shadow organizations for support, and they move into full-blown workaholism themselves.

Recovering work addicts have learned that if their sobriety is their focus, and if they live honestly and spiritually, the rest of their lives take care of themselves. Organizations that attend to producing a quality product with integrity find that the bottom line takes care of itself.

Short-Term Solution, Short-Term Rewards

Workaholics have monotone minds, workaholic organizations have myopic minds. They go for the fix of the short-term solution rather than risk the long-term plan. An aspect of the workaholic's dishonesty is impression management. They look good on the outside, while chaos rages inside. The workaholic's family gets hooked into the same process. Rather than risking an intervention that will have long-range consequences, they placate. They look for ways to get through each situation.

Workaholic organizations are frantic organizations. They rush around, they change strategies, they feel confused. They leap to solutions without thinking through the implications. Think of how exhausting this is for people who work there. The addict is not predictable, so the loved ones become hypervigilant. The organization is not predictable, and people are kept on their toes.

Ironically, short-term solutions almost always have long-term consequences, so the time saved now is multiplied a hundredfold in cleaning up the mess down the line. Surely this has been the lesson we are learning from environmental pollution.

On a cargo freighter traveling from Antwerp to Montreal, I saw an example of short-term thinking. Cargo freighters are one of the fastest growing transport industries in the world. Every day billions of tons of goods are transported on the seas by massive freighters. I was astounded at the speed with which the freighter was loaded and the efficiency with which it was guided through harbors and locks. But piled on the lower deck was a mountain of crates, boxes, plastic, Styrofoam, and garbage soiling an otherwise spotless vessel. I was told that neither port would remove trash, that the freighter company had attempted to contract for trash removal, and had been denied. The solution? Dump trash in the ocean. Every day this freighter and hundreds of others dump trash. It has been going on for years and will, no doubt, continue. Antwerp, the port from which we departed, is the second-largest cargo port in the world. It has the technology to load one ship with 28,000 tons of cargo in *twenty-four* hours, but it does not use its technology to remove a few hundred pounds of garbage. Instead freighters pollute the very highway of ocean that so graciously carries them from port to port, from dollar to dollar. Who can calculate the effects on the complex ecosystem under the sea? Only an addict obsessed with the god illusion would dare tamper with it, and this is the stupidity of the myopic workaholic organization.

Mission Denied

Although I write about the addictive aspects of organizations, I nevertheless persist in my belief in organizations. I still believe in the power of corporate effort. I happen to feel that together we can do more than any one of us alone. I have this hope because my own life is filled with extraordinary experiences in organizations where the missions are sacred trusts. The mission is the reason for their existence, their purpose in being. Without a sense of mission, organizations are soulless.

Unfortunately, the workaholic organization has usually lost sight of its mission. It may give lip service to the mission, but in reality something else has replaced it, usually a preoccupation with profit. The workaholic loses self in the progress of the disease. The workaholic's identity is the disease. This is why some addicts exhibit a schizophrenic personality. When they are involved in the addiction, they become someone else.

Workaholic organizations are inevitably out of touch with their mission. In stages, they ignore the mission, it fades, it doesn't inform decision making. Eventually, it doesn't matter any more. Something else is driving the company.

Workaholic organizations rarely do internally what they do well in the marketplace. For example, I have worked with many hospitals. Their mission is healing. Yet some of the most unhealthy people I encounter are doctors and nurses. I have several church organizations as clients. I rarely find spirituality among church professionals. Telephone companies' most serious internal problems are with communications.

Imagine the stress on workers that workaholic organizations create by being out of sync with the mission. If people join organizations to help heal, communicate, invent, and so on, and they find themselves not doing the very thing that drew them there in the first place, it creates tremendous stress.

Workaholic organizations let conflicts of interest deter

them from their mission. They prefer to spend time focused on the conflict rather than their real purpose.

An architectural firm that was designing a building for its own company entered into a conflict of interest between landscapers and engineers. The landscapers wanted clear windows in the entry atrium (for plants), and the engineers wanted tinted glass to conserve heat and cooling. The landscapers won.

Three receptionists sit in the atrium. All day the sun beats down on their heads. They have resorted to wearing sunglasses, large straw hats, and encasing their computer screens in cardboard to shade the glare. They are irritable and cross due to the intense heat and the working conditions. Now, these three women are the first people prospective clients meet upon entering the building. The receptionists and the atrium are the firm's advertisement for the type of architectural work they offer!

As a last resort, the firm erected three large beach umbrellas over each receptionist to shield them from the heat. A prospective client confided to me that he thought he had the wrong address when he entered the building. "I thought maybe I had mistakenly walked into some kind of upscale travel agency, where the agents dress for the beach!" The company's motto was, "We design environments for people!"

Workaholic organizations cannot keep their priorities straight. Without clear direction from their mission they make everything hard. The simplest tasks become onerous because they have no clear path. Think of the toll on employees and customers alike.

Crisis Management Is the Norm

Workaholic organizations leap from crisis to crisis. The crisis infuses a false energy into people. It creates an environment in which the usual rules are suspended and extraordinary processes take over.

I recently encountered a book that advocates creating crisis as a management principle. The author reflected on the fact that, in crisis, people put aside their usual animosities. They pull together, they are selfless, and they expend extra effort. They also get a high from getting through the experience. His book counsels managers to develop the conditions under which people are responding with extraordinary dedication. This is called peak performance.

I call it prescription for burnout. Any stress expert can tell us the rudimentary facts of burnout. When the adrenals are constantly producing adrenaline, they eventually give out. When the adrenals give out, you give out. Meeting crisis after crisis exhausts the adrenals.

In connection with the crisis orientation, it is necessary to look at the role of stress-management seminars as one method by which workaholic organizations protect their addiction. Ordinarily, stress-management is a training workshop in which employees are given instruments to measure their degree of stress. Then they are introduced to theories of stress (such as fight-flight); taught relaxation techniques; and counseled about the importance of nutrition and exercise in reducing stress. The dominant message is, "You are responsible for taking hold of your life and handling stress." Never do stress workshops point to the origins of stress in the organization: management and the workaholic corporate culture. Subtly, stress workshops imply that the employee is to blame for being stressed out. Yet, a large amount of stress actually comes from management policy, style, and climate—all of which are heavily laden with crisis.

Besides the danger inherent to workers and organizations in the crisis mode, there is a deeper question: Why is it that people must be pumped up to do their work? Why does the organization feel it has to do something to them to get them to perform? Why isn't the mission of the organization, combined with the skill of the employee and the cooperation of co-workers, enough?

I believe that in healthy organizations the challenge of their mission and the integrity of their process is enough. They don't need techniques for interesting people in work. The environment provides sufficient real events (some of them crisis) that there isn't a need to make artificial ones.

Workaholic organizations are crisis-ridden and crisis creators. This is because the addictive process is a process of confusion. The crisis serves to keep everyone busy and away from asking those deeper questions that could lead to recovery and healing.

No Boundaries, No Respect

Workaholic organizations know no limits. Sometimes they get greedy. They launch projects that are ill-prepared. They follow the crowd. Immersed in the illusion of control and perfectionism, they have no respect for themselves. Their lack of respect extends to workers.

A boundary is a line. When an organization respects boundaries, it knows the difference between itself and something else. And it doesn't enter something else unless invited.

The workaholic organization and the workaholic employee have very flimsy boundaries. The major complaint of work addicts' families is that work spills over into every area of domestic life. There are no boundaries protecting them from the addict's fix. The major complaint of employees in workaholic organizations is that the organization has no respect for their personal, private lives. The workaholic organization expects to be first in your life and acts accordingly. There are several technologies that facilitate the invasion of the corporate into the private.

The telephone and electronic mail are both ways of contacting employees day and night. For the work addict, these two technologies are the paraphernalia of the addiction. You can be kept busy and you can keep others hopping by the use of electronic mail (a device on which you can leave messages twenty-four hours a day and pick them up at your leisure), or by calling them on the phone. As time becomes our most precious commodity, we find more people needing cellular phones so they are never away from phone contact. Several corporations have had to develop policies to regulate electronic mail, because they found the workaholics in the company were using it day and night. Other employees could not enjoy a holiday without anxiety that an important message was waiting.

An elderly diplomat spoke to me poignantly about how out of it he felt when he recently returned to the United States after thirty years in the foreign service. Reflecting on the evolution of the briefcase, he said, "When I entered the diplomatic corps the only thing we carried to work was a small sack with a lunch in it. Then people began carrying briefcases, but they were only status symbols. If they contained anything other than an umbrella, the contents were never looked at. They were just carried back and forth from work. Now people's briefcases are bulging, they work at home, and more than that many have computers there as well."

What the diplomat observed is a testimony to the speed of change. The technology is neither good nor bad. It exists. But having the technology allows us powerful tools that can now be used in the service of the addictive process, and can become addicting in themselves.

Developing clear boundaries, knowing when to say "No, you can come this far but no farther," is a crucial aspect of a workaholic's recovery. Organizations also have responsibilities in this area. It is not their prerogative to run rampant into every minute of an employee's life. They have a responsibility to set boundaries for themselves and to respect others' rights to a life separate from work.

Workaholic Characteristics in the Organization

Many of the characteristics found in the individual work addict are also found in the workaholic organization.

Organizations usually suffer *multiple addictions*. If workaholism is the primary, unquestioned addiction in the company, one can be sure there are backup addictions supporting it. Many companies use alcohol and food to take the edge off the pain of working so hard and to reward people for their extra effort. Some organizations are in an addictive relationship with certain suppliers, and refuse to dump them even when more qualified and economical alternatives exist. Money addiction goes hand in hand with work addiction. Obsessing about the bottom line of the financial statement and putting profits before quality and people all contribute to the addictive nature of the organization.

Almost all workaholic organizations are into some form of *denial*. Their denial takes the form of boasting about productivity, while remaining silent about the effects on people. They alter the financial data so it does not look as bad as it is. They are *dishonest* about their products and their place in relation to competitors. Like the individual work addict, who struggles with *self-esteem*, the organization can have trouble seeing itself honestly. These organizations exaggerate their successes and brood over failures. They are *self-centered*, believing that everything that happens in the world economy and their own markets is a direct assault on them.

Workaholic organizations are *judgmental* about themselves. They overreact to changes, seeing each one as a crisis, not an opportunity. Compulsive organizations look outside themselves to understand their process. They frequently look for others to blame rather than take responsibility within. Workaholic organizations are *punishing* organizations, and it is dangerous for individuals to own up to mistakes. Consequently, everyone is shifting blame to someone else. Moreover, workaholic organizations use *external measures* as the sole criterion of success. Feeling good is related to doing tasks well. In this paradigm, learning is one-dimensional. It is always about external success.

Workaholic organizations *never relax*. They resist stepping back to evaluate or reconsider a direction. They feel driven. Employees joke about working half-days — 8 A.M. to 8 P.M. Work-addicted organizations define success in terms of change and the new. Recently, a man in our training group wore a tee-shirt that proclaimed, "When you are standing on the edge of a cliff, progress can be defined as taking one step backwards."

The workaholic organization does not understand this concept. They are frequently in *crisis mode*. In fact, crisis is a way of life in these companies. Crises are used to suspend the usual corporate rules and to get extra effort out of people. Initially, the crises are sporadic. As the company sinks further into its work addiction, crises are part and parcel of the usual operating procedure. People begin to define the crisis mentality as normal and as "just the way it is around here." Crisis is only one form of control for these organizations. Control pervades the company. The workaholic pace controls workers; the unrealistic deadlines control quality; and fatigue eventually controls the final output. Finally, these qualities lead into the *perfectionistic* organization.

I dare say, many of us would like to see more quality coming out of American corporations, but perfectionism may not be the way to go. In the perfectionistic organization humanness is not allowed to flourish. Work is repeated over and over until just right; rarely does the workaholic organization discriminate between projects that should be done "just so," and projects that can be let go. The margin for error is exceedingly slim.

Finally, workaholic organizations experience little internal *intimacy*. Most relationships are superficial. Feelings are not allowed and are rarely expressed openly. Exceptions to this are fear and anger, two feelings that are used to intimidate and motivate others.

Styles of Work Addiction in the Organization

Some organizations exhibit distinctive styles of work addiction. On the whole, the most pervasive style is the *compulsive, relentless, driven* organization. Its management style and personnel policies are designed to get more out of people by occupying them with endless tasks.

Other organizations resemble the *binge* worker. Often organizations devoted to short-term goals are like a workaholic on a binge. Some organizations operate normally for a while, and suddenly go whole hog after new projects. A recent case is a school for exceptional children that had been developing its curriculum carefully over many years. The school hired a new director, a dynamic workaholic who led the school into a series of disastrous binges. The director himself was binging on exercise and wilderness activities. He convinced the staff that wilderness programs should be at the core of the curriculum. For several years wilderness was the chief emphasis; but instead of being a welcome addition to the course of studies, it took over the entire curriculum. It also kept everyone so busy surviving the trips that they rarely dealt with internal conflicts among themselves or with the director. Nor did they have to face the drudgery and discipline of less active studies. Three years later, the director started on a nutrition binge and attempted to direct the school accordingly. At this point, some faculty woke up. They did an intervention with the director, which enabled him to confront his work addiction and got the school into a more balanced position.

One would think that a work-*anorexic* organization would go out of business quickly. Indeed, I saw one such organization struggle mightily to stay afloat. Work-anorexic organizations spent inordinate hours planning the work so as to avoid the work. A construction cooperative in the Northwest operated in an anorexic fashion. The company was committed to quality housing that was energy efficient. The company was cooperatively owned by all the employees. At first the group spent six months developing its mission and business plan. Although the members wanted to work cooperatively with one another, they actually avoided conflict instead of negotiating conflicts. A by-product of their avoidance was that they developed eight pages of guiding values by which to govern the company instead of a few workable principles. The internal strife continues, with the result that when they do get contracts they feel rushed to perform and they are often late in finishing projects. In these times they put an SOS out to the entire co-op and everyone pulls together, thus giving themselves the illusion that they can work well when they have to. Today the venture is still on shaky ground. It has never been as profitable as it could be, because members insist on reworking the value statements rather than getting on with the construction projects.

Closet workaholic organizations always have one more thing waiting in the wings. While the closet worker hides his or her stash, the organization mysteriously comes up with projects employees haven't bargained for. Employees in closet organizations complain that their job descriptions rarely contain all the things that are expected of them. Many people in the helping professions find that the extras that go with the job are often more time consuming than the job itself.

Even consultants fall into the disease of the closet worker organization. I once was hired to design an evaluation process for the president of a company. In the course of developing the process, the evaluation committee confided that, in addition to the evaluation, they had another job for me. As long as I was going to be around the company, would I mediate a longstanding conflict between two managers? Unfortunately, this request was made before I began my recovery from my codependency. I was so happy to be asked and so determined to please them that of course I agreed to their request. I discovered too late that the conflict between the managers was far more difficult a task than the evaluation process. It took time, energy, and thinking that should rightfully have gone into the job I was hired to do. I worked myself ragged and probably did a halfway job on both items. It was a very expensive lesson for me and did not help the organization in the long run.

Like the individual workaholic, organizations share one, two, some, or all of these characteristics and styles. Many of these practices we have deemed "normal" and just a part of the usual business practice. As I work in addictive organizations, I see that what we have called normal is really the disease process of the addictive system. When it is in the form of workaholism, it is even more difficult to recognize. Nevertheless, employees increasingly have vague feelings that something is just not right. Even when they cannot name what is going on they feel the dis-ease. These inklings are the beginning of naming the workaholic organization in its various forms.

Hooked on All the Myths about Workaholism

Workaholic organizations are into the addictive process to the extent that they have bought into all the myths about workaholism. They believe workaholism is profitable to the corporation, so they reward and encourage work-addicted behavior. They feature "happy workaholics" in the company newsletter. They believe work addiction is a positive addiction, so they send employees to seminars for the purpose of making them more productive. They think workaholism only adversely affects the workaholic, so they privatize the disease by sending burned-out employees to EAP (Employee Assistance Programs) counselors. They don't deal with burnout as symptomatic of the entire corporation. They believe workaholism can be managed with stress-reduction techniques, so they sponsor corporate gyms and workshops on stress management. They believe workaholism only affects high-powered executives, so many of the stress-reduction perks are only available to that group. They believe no one ever died of hard work, so they routinely develop job descriptions that are beyond the reach of those doing them.

Overall, the workaholic organization needs workaholics to survive; and, conversely, employees must become workaholic to survive in these companies. For the new breed of corporate men and women, the corporation is the new church and workaholism is the religion.

Usually, people who begin their recovery from their workaholism cannot remain in workaholic organizations. They need all the support they can get. By the same token, we need to see that workaholic organizations are sick organizations. They have a disease and they also need help. Every workaholic who recovers takes step one out of the disease. Organizations too can recover—and they owe it to their mission, their employees, and their consumers to do their part in recognizing their part in this problem and doing something about it.

The Economics of Workaholism

Workaholism is a hidden disease that is only recently being named in corporations, so gathering hard data on the economic consequences to corporations is difficult. However, according to many CEOs and managers, this disease is costing mightily.

The evidence is that tired workers make more mistakes, spend extra time redoing mistakes, and have a higher incidence of accidents. The more technical the jobs, the more likely that workaholism manifests itself as a "psychological disorder," like depression or another addiction problem. In fact, according to the National Council on Compensation Insurance, psychological problems are one of the fastest-growing occupational ills since 1980.

Stress, which is a side effect of workaholism, now accounts for 14 percent of occupational disease—a change from 1980, when stress accounted for less than 5 percent. There are no figures for the total cost of stress diseases, but the average claim for medical and benefit payments is $15,000, or twice as much as that paid to workers with physical injuries. Moreover, workers are now suing companies over stress-related diseases. Paul Rosch, president of the American Institute of Stress, says that ten years ago hardly anyone heard of workers being compensated for other than physical diseases. Now the number of claims is growing. "As precedents are set for worker's compensation, the situation is only going to get worse," said Rosch.

It would be in the interests of corporations to address the issue of all the addictive diseases, especially workaholism, so as to avoid facing claims like the one brought in Oregon. The president of a Globe Machine subsidiary insisted that the stress of managing a company in bankruptcy led him back to alcoholism. He sued the parent company and won.

From another perspective, personnel departments calculate the cost of replacing a burned-out employee to be two to three times the employee's annual salary. The lost time before the employee leaves, the time without a replacement, and the cost of replacing and retraining all amount to a constant financial and energy drain on the corporation.

Then there is the issue of productivity. It has yet to be proven that the longer a worker toils, the more productive he or she is. The evidence seems to be to the contrary. The president of a midsized electronics assembly plant related his approach to dealing with a workaholic employee. His employee insisted upon working twelve hours a day. Although discouraged by supervisors, he was driven to excessive working by his workaholism. Finally, the president used drastic measures and took the man's plant keys away from him. At five o'clock he was literally locked out of the building. Initially, the employee was disgruntled and seemed lost and confused. However, after two weeks, the company president noticed that the employee's productivity was higher for his forty-hour week than it had been in his sixty-hour week. His heightened productivity has remained constant, benefiting both the worker and the company.

The prognosis is not good for organizations that have significant numbers of workaholics on their payroll. There is hope, however. Workaholism is a disease whose basic addictive structure is well understood and highly treatable. For organizations that begin to confront this problem, complete recovery is possible—a claim that cannot be made about many other diseases.

If it is possible to make a clarion call to the corporate community, I make it here. Workaholism is a deadly disease. It is in exactly the opposite direction from where corporate America says it wants to go to regain its place in the world market. The onus of healing cannot rest with individual workaholics alone. True, they must take responsibility for their lives and actions; but organizations bear responsibility for this disease as well. To the extent they foster it, promote it, and reward it, organizations have responsibility for healing themselves and then becoming healthy places to work. The lives of individuals depend upon it; so does the society.

10. Why Are We Doing This to Ourselves?

I am on a cargo freighter in the North Atlantic Sea, 1,200 miles from Antwerp and 1,500 miles from Montreal, my destination. We have hit a low-pressure weather system. Dense fog and drizzle surround our massive ship. We lumber over large ocean swells. We press on.

I am on the bridge deck, the place from which the ship is navigated. I am peering into impenetrable grayness and I am pondering work addiction and American society. There seems as thick a veil of denial surrounding this disease as the fog shrouding the ship.

I stand there as the gray turns into the night and I question why, as a society, we are so slow in naming work addiction a fatal disease. Why has it stayed hidden for so long, not talked about or taken seriously? It is so pervasive and we are so silent . . . we are only as sick as the secrets we keep.

Then I remember an experiment with frogs. It goes like this. If you drop a frog into a pot of boiling water, it will leap out immediately. But if you put a frog in a pot of cool water and gradually heat the water to the boiling point, it will remain in the pot until it dies. I think this is the metaphor for workaholism in our society.

Workaholism has become so common, so accepted in the society, that we do not realize we are in a pot reaching the boiling point. Moreover, the very nature of the addictive process is to numb our awareness of the addictive process itself. So, the longer the pot heats up (the addiction continues), the more unlikely it is we have the needed resources (presence of mind) to jump out.

Increasing numbers of social commentators have begun to note our growing disengagement from our own dilemma. They give us a better idea of why we tolerate workaholism so willingly.

The most knowledgeable writer on the issues of addiction and society is Anne Wilson Schaef. She shifted our perspective from addiction as a solely individual pathology to the fact that there is an underlying addictive process in the society at large.[1] This underlying addictive process supports individual addictions and is larger than individual addictions.

Schaef observes the society and concludes that not only does it support addictions, it actively promotes them. One has only to look at advertising, listen to music, and observe the political scene to be aware of the truth of her observation.

Futurist Harlan Ellison, who stars in ads for the Geo line of auto imports from General Motors, made a similar point in a speech before the Western States Advertising Agencies Association:

> Your children use drugs, and you told them to do it. You've been pushing chemicals on TV for years: "Can't sleep? Take a drug. Not happy? Take a drug." Where in the world did people get the idea that it's smart to get in a car and go fast? To get in a 4-by-4 and tear up virgin land? You told them to do it. As much as you are subject to the whims of your deranged clients, you rule the world. You have the reins to the most powerful medium in the world—television. And the only people who can afford to advertise on television are the lowest common denominator of goods.[2]

Schaef believes that the norm for the society is the addictive process. It is not that we have a society that is relatively healthy, and off to one side is a small pocket of addicts who are dysfunctional. No, the society itself operates out of an illusionary reality, which it calls reality but is really an addictive process. Why is this so? Schaef says it is so because the best-adjusted person in our society is the person who is not dead and who is not fully alive—the zombie, the numb.

If you are dead, you cannot do the work of the society; if you are fully alive, you resist many of the processes of the society. When you are fully alive, you let yourself feel the pain of living in an environment where we pollute our water and air, where we risk nuclear annihilation, where relationships are fragmented, and so on. Schaef realizes that we live in a society fraught with pain and contradiction and emptiness. The addictive process, she feels, puts a buffer between ourselves and those feelings. It takes us out of touch. We get so busy with our individual addictions that we don't have to move to the deeper questions. We lose ourselves and then we are malleable in the addictive society.[3]

Lawrence Chickering, writing in the *Wall Street Journal*, makes the same point as Schaef. He believes the anti-drug policy in the United States is doomed to failure because it is based on an antiquated view of social policy—blaming the suppliers. He argues that the strategy our government has chosen—"vigorous criminal prosecution of suppliers—is the centerpiece of the codependent spirit that animates our national policy toward drugs and makes it *impossible to have a serious policy on addiction.*"[4] (Italics mine.) And then Chickering makes the key point, one that I doubt the regular readers of the *Wall Street Journal* wish to confront:

> Most important, however, is the fact that almost everyone ignores—and, I will argue, even *denies*—the much more troublesome psychological issue of demand: why large numbers of people in all social and economic classes choose to anesthetize themselves regularly from the experiences of ordinary life.[5]

Unfortunately for great numbers of people, the experiences of ordinary life are experiences of racism, sexism, class-ism, ageism, adultism, abuse, loneliness, and meaningless-ness. "Love and nurturing are necessary for individuals to become fully functional. Addictive behavior is an effort to deny the painful reality of their absence."[6]

If ever a society wanted the perfect addiction, it is worka-holism. It is the ideal response to the addictive society because it is an acceptable form of adaptation to an insane world. Just as family members adjust their behavior to the active addict in the family, the workaholic adjusts to the organization and the society. The adaptation may appear healthy and stable to the outside observer, but the stability is not the equivalent of functional behavior; it is merely a pat-terned response to a dysfunctional situation.[7]

In the family, codependents look good. They are long-suffering. They hang in there when others opt out. They are loyal and understanding. Unfortunately, these very behaviors are undermining because they prevent the addict and the dys-functional family from falling on their faces and getting the help they need.

In the addictive society, the workaholic is both addict and codependent. He or she suffers a disease and thereby con-tinues support of addictive institutions. The institutions in turn are driven by scores of workaholics, and also use them to stay in their dysfunctional process. The match is so complete that it looks to be a situation of equilibrium. Is it any wonder that those who are recovering from addictions seriously ask themselves if they are crazy upon encountering these worka-holic institutions? In reality, if foreign competitors were creeping into US factories and spraying a numbing nerve gas at workers, they could not be more effective than the addictive process of workaholism.

The society needs workaholism to stay in the addictive process. Given the fact that the addictive process is cunning, baffling, powerful, and patient, it will develop even more sophisticated forms of addiction. Workaholism is surely one of those.

How Our Institutions Support Work Addiction

Work addiction doesn't just float around in the air. It is embodied and supported. Three of our hallowed institutions are prime supporters of the disease: the educational system, the church, and the political system. I know there are many others, but I believe these three have been major contributors to the development of a workaholic ethic as distinct from a work ethic.

The Educational System

The processes in many of our educational systems are such that they require children either to work addictively or to fail. Educators are raising the alarm at the early age youngsters are expected to perform as little perfectionists. They decry the relentless scheduling of every hour of youngsters' time. The result is that children never learn to organize their own time, nor to respect their own preferences and rhythms. They are constantly responding to something outside themselves.

We should carefully consider the experience of the Japanese, whose children are under great pressure to get into the best schools so they can get the right job in the best company. Japan has the highest rate of teenage suicide in the world.

Colleges and universities in the United States are the training ground for the addictive organization. Students are expected to take a certain number of hours of courses. They complain that the amount of work for the courses is not humanly possible to accomplish. The majority of college students now work in addition to going to school. The relentless pressure they feel often results in serious doubts about their competency and ability, and hence in lowered self-esteem.

A student personnel director said she felt that the role of student personnel offices was to create excellence in students by urging them to excel beyond what they felt they could do. When I questioned her about students who weren't sleeping and barely stopping to eat, she replied that was typical of student life. All college kids live that way in these years. In addition, such processes as honors and getting A's were ways of pushing kids and giving them tangible evidence that they were better than their peers.

We might even question the quarter system, which is popular in a number of universities. This is the practice of having four three-month quarters of classes instead of the old semester system, which extended study over two long periods with a shorter summer session in between. One young woman confided that the quarter system was so intense that "you must begin studying hard right away, and if you get sick or have to be away for a week, forget it. You can never make up the amount of work you missed."

Eager to learn more about the climate in colleges today, I asked a group of teachers and students if there wasn't time for contemplation and meditation. After all, wasn't this the idea of the university? A place to think about great ideas? They laughed politely, and I feel sure they thought I was nuts! The teachers are under the same pressure as the students. They are expected to teach more hours and publish more articles. Students dash from class to work, and my ideal of faculty and students sitting around exchanging ideas is quite rare.

Work addiction extends through the ranks of all teachers, from elementary to university. A typical study of elementary and junior high teachers showed that 56 percent had tendencies toward workaholism, as measured by two scales. In both groups, over half were experiencing burnout due to school climate and feelings of depersonalization.[8]

Clearly, workaholism is not solely the addiction of high-powered executives. Children are being trained for it from preschool. The processes of external pressures, comparison, more work than is possible in the time allotted, and adult models who are frantic and harried—all of these educational characteristics tell children that work addiction is to be imitated. Moreover, it gives the impression that workaholism is normal. Workaholic expectations create tremendous pressures on youngsters. It is no wonder, then, that drug and alcohol use begin at such an early age. The pain of working so hard must find blessed relief in the numbness of a drink or a drug. Our educational institutions are plagued with problems, not the least being workaholism, the new pedagogy.

The Church

There is a lot of debate today about whether we can trace workaholism's roots to the Protestant work ethic, to Puritanism, and to Calvinism. I am not so sure we can trace work addiction to these theologies, because I think workaholism is part of a wider disease process in the society. I will leave that debate to the theologians. Whatever the historical roots of work addiction are, however, it is pervasive in our society and rampant in the church. Actually, I find the church's style of workaholism one of the most seductive forms of the disease.

The church, in its training of ministers and in its practice, actively promotes work addictions. The good Christian or Jew is someone who works hard on behalf of others, never counting the cost to self or family. In fact, in many theologies, it is considered selfish to attend to your own needs. Countless priests, ministers, rabbis, and nuns have said that the explicit message they received in their training was that they had been given a special "call" by God to serve others. They were ordained to serve. Others' needs should always come before their own. To act differently amounted to blasphemy.

This notion of call has been a heavy burden for professional church people, and I have encountered many ministers who have bitterly denounced the concept of call. They have experienced it as theologically sanctioned workaholism, which also receives the wholehearted support of parishioners.

Pastors and rabbis are expected to sacrifice themselves and their families. Churches think nothing of asking them to work seventy, eighty, or even ninety hours a week, although the Alban Institute believes fifty-five hours per week is the maximum a pastor can work and still be effective. I remember a workshop for professional church workers in which I was sharing some of my ideas about work addiction. I met the greatest resistance from the ministers. Exasperated, one of them blurted out, "It's not OK to kill myself for work, but it is OK to kill myself for Christ." I asked him to consider why God needed his workaholism, and to check out the idolatry of *his* god illusion. Needless to say, I was not invited back to that group!

Spouses and friends of professional church workers often suffer, receiving only the dregs of leftover energy from their loved one. A clergy wife related a common experience. Her husband was a prominent pastor in an urban church. He was very effective in his ministry and popular with the people. But his wife felt she never really knew him. She said she learned more about him when he preached than she did when they related one-to-one. This pastor's intimacy was with his work. In his work, he was able to keep control. In his relationship with his wife, he was not able to control their interactions; she brought up things he wasn't ready for or felt uncomfortable discussing. He avoided intimacy with her with the excuse he was too busy, while appearing to be intimate in the setting of the church, where he was in control of how others saw him. Given the stress of church occupations, coupled with the institutional support for workaholism, it is not surprising that ministers, priests, rabbis, and nuns have one of the highest rates of disability in the nation. The insurance claims due to stress and addictions are greater than in almost any other segment of the population.

Church groups need to ask themselves how they can expect church leaders to be creative and multiskilled, yet not allow time for study leave, reading, and yes, even prayer. None of these activities is seen as really working.

Blind devotion to keeping busy keeps us out of touch with what is really going on in our churches. Even those who become addicted to causes (causeaholics) lose themselves with the excuse that a cause for the poor and oppressed justifies the self-abuse of the addiction. In all honesty, church workaholics need to break through this basic denial: They run themselves ragged in the guise of good work.

This is an end-and-means problem for the churches. Because the end is a "good work," all sorts of activities are justified and go unexamined. But when the process by which you reach the end is an addictive process, the eventual result is a loss of spirituality. This is one reason why any addiction, but especially work addiction, is so deadly for the churches. "Doing" religion workaholically is an assault on the very spirituality the church promises. How can you teach "life and life more abundant" when you are working yourself to death?

There has been a steady loss of membership from the mainline Protestant churches in the United States, while the fundamentalist churches are growing. I don't believe fundamentalists are less work addicted than mainline churches; I do believe that people seek meaning and spirituality in their churches. They seek an alternative to the dominant societal culture. No business organization promises you your soul—they promise you salary, benefits, retirement, and perhaps status, if it is a fine company. The church, however, promises spirituality and instead gives workaholism.

No church hiring committee would consider giving a job to an applicant who was an active drug abuser. Why hire an active workaholic? Same disease, same consequences, same loss of spirituality. But churches not only hire workaholics all the time, they actively seek them. And then they use people up instead of examining their addictive structures. This is a moral issue the churches are not facing.

I believe the active support for workaholism, which pervades the churches, extends to the church members, who are naturally in despair that they cannot find in church or society an oasis of sanity, a place where authentic spirituality is possible. Moreover, the theology and modeling by clergy supports the church members in their work addiction.

No one is exempt from the problem of workaholism. The monk, Thomas Merton, writing thirty-seven years ago, said:

> I have fallen into the great indignity I have written against—I am a contemplative who is ready to collapse from overwork. This, I think, is a sin and the punishment of sin but now I have got to turn it to good use and be a saint by it, somehow.[9]

Because our society is an addictive system, all institutions are affected. Therefore it is unlikely that the church would be exempt from workaholism. The recovery from workaholism has so much to offer the churches. Workaholics are great controllers and ultimate perfectionists—two qualities not found in the godlike. Think of the renaissance if people could look to the church as a place of rest, nurture, and justice rather than a treadmill of frantic activity.

The Political System

I meet very few people who are not cynical about our political system and its leaders. In the 1988 election campaign, both Democrats and Republicans were exasperated and embarrassed by the nonsubstantial campaigns waged by both candidates. Those who participate actively in our government act "as if" the process makes sense. Anyone who knows about the addictive process in families understands that we are seeing in our political system the dynamics of denial, dishonesty, and dysfunction.

The entire political process is an addictive process. It is supported by drug, alcohol, money, relationship, and sex addictions to name a few. Its pervasive addiction, workaholism, characterizes almost all of its activities.

For example, the individual workaholic leaps for the short-term solution. He or she goes for the immediate fix. The 1980s were characterized by exactly this kind of thinking. Instead of investing in the future, which would be investing in education, research, environment, and the country's infrastructure, we experienced supply-side economics, Contra aid, arms to Iran, financial manipulation, and deficit spending. Consequently, our highways and bridges are falling apart, pollution is a life-threatening problem, and our educational system is lagging behind.

Workaholism is progressive and fatal. What is the arms race if not a race toward madness? Workaholics exhaust themselves with intense effort. As a result, they lose sight of their real priorities. This has been the story of our stockpiling of an arsenal of arms far in excess of anything we could ever need.

Kurt Vonnegut calls those who think this way "weapons junkies." He said,

> I am persuaded that there are among us people who are tragically hooked on preparations for war. Tell people with that disease that war is coming and we have to get ready for it, and for a few minutes there they will be as happy as a drunk with his martini breakfast or a compulsive gambler with his paycheck bet on the Super Bowl.[10]

Vonnegut goes on to say that we the people have contributed to this tragedy because of our ignorance of the disease. As a result, we have entrusted power to people we did not know were sickies. But this is exactly the terrible paradigm workaholism exhibits. Because *we are addicted,* we give power to those like ourselves. We lose our sense of judgment and feel comfortable in the presence of the disease.

Some have pointed to the defeat of John Tower as Secretary of Defense as a sign of growing awareness of alcoholism among our political leaders. Yet the Bush administration battled to the end to save Tower's nomination, even when they had information that he could put away a bottle of Johnny Walker Red at one sitting two or three nights a week. Even the notion that Tower could "stay on the wagon" was trivialized by the press, and one *Washington Post* writer compared Tower's pledge to abstain from alcohol, if confirmed, as "akin to Count Dracula pledging to switch to Gatorade—if he'd just be allowed to drive the bloodmobile."[11]

So, Tower was defeated; and waiting in the wings was Bush's next nominee, Dick Cheney, a workaholic. Cheney was described as the "pragmatist whom every president needs." I believe a more accurate description is that Cheney was the more acceptable addict.

Forty-eight years old, Cheney came to the White House having had three heart attacks, starting at the age of thirty-seven, when he was running for Congress. After his last heart-bypass surgery at age forty-eight, he returned to work within three weeks of the operation. A dedicated public servant, he once worked six months straight with only one day off.

Cheney appears to have the same addictive process disease as Tower, only a different form of it. Yet he easily passed Congressional confirmation for Secretary of Defense.

Through the whole Tower-Cheney fiasco, the denial process remained intact. The congress and the press insisted that Tower was defeated for political reasons. And the Bush administration was reported to have said, "The fastest way to get this debacle behind us is to come up with a well-respected nominee as fast as we can." Can there be any doubt that workaholism is the cleanest of all the addictions?

Finally, what about the politics of drugs? I believe our failure to deal with the drug problem arises from the fact that we attempt solutions that are themselves addictive processes,

workaholic solutions. A few cases: Workaholics have difficulty setting priorities, so they launch out on projects that are
counterproductive to one another. They have lost the capacity
for knowing what is really important. The same system of
confused thinking enables Congress to subsidize the tobacco
industry, whose product, nicotine, is responsible for 390,000
deaths annually, while also funding cancer research. The
funding of lung cancer research is a form of impression management, because the data is already in: Lung cancer is pre-
ventable if you stop smoking.

The case of street drugs shows another side of workaholic
functioning. Comedienne Whoopi Goldberg has noted that
she is constantly surprised that every thirteen-year-old resi-
dent of the inner city knows who the drug dealers are, but the
police don't. Why is this?

I believe it is due to the politics of dysfunction. Addictions
are system diseases, therefore addictions can be used to support some interests against others. Addictions blunt our feelings and our awareness. What would our inner-city residents
be doing if they were in touch with the pain of their homeless-
ness and joblessness? I think they would be angry and the cities would be burning. For those who wish to preserve the
current imbalance of power, a drugged, numbed population is
easier to manipulate than an aware, furious one.

This is the social systems dimension of workaholism: Our
approach to resolving the drug problem is workaholic,
because the very purpose of our efforts is to keep us from solv-
ing the problem.

Ineffective action is the hallmark of the workaholic society. In a very real way, we are attempting to fight an addiction
to drugs with an addictive process. The disease meets the disease and, like a hurricane gathering force, leaves destruction
in its wake.

Many workaholics describe the experience of running as
hard as they can through work, while feeling they are going

backward. They get further and further behind. This is our experience with the war on drugs. The furious activity gives us the illusion of progress and dulls our awareness that we aren't even standing still. We are going backward.

Twelve-Step addictions recovery programs have maintained that because addictions are progressive, there is no such thing as standing still. You are either going forward or going back. I believe that is the case with drugs in our society: It is obvious that we are slipping. Unfortunately, the entire political process seems mired in the addictive process. The use of workaholism as a remedy ("work harder to fix it") is exactly the wrong remedy. In fact, it promises to sink us deeper.

Social Implications

The thorough integration of workaholism into our society results in a complete hologram: The individual is the family is the organization is the society. These elements don't just mirror one another, they *are* one another. Workaholism is a deadly, dangerous disease because the individual feels so comfortable in it wherever he or she goes. There is no dissonance in this disease. It feels "normal" and indeed it is "normal" in an illusionary, addictive society.

The longer the addictive process goes unnamed in the society, the more sophisticated it becomes. The more sophisticated, the "trickier" the disease process. I believe workaholism is a clear barometer of the trickiness of the disease. The integration of workaholism into our essential institutions—education, church, politics—indicates its power.

The pervasiveness of workaholic thinking makes recovery from this and any addictive disease quite difficult. In the case of workaholism, there is active support for the disease in the society and little or no support for recovery.

There is another implication of workaholism that we rarely consider. Because work addiction keeps us busy, we stay estranged from our essential selves. An aspect of that estrangement is that we cease asking ourselves if we are doing our right work. Are we actually performing the task or pursuing the vocation we need to be doing? Is it good for us, for our families, and the universe? I believe the social implication of workaholism is that we don't ask the questions for two reasons: (1) We aren't doing our true work, and (2) in our society, few people have access to their right work. In the addictive society, you cannot afford to ask the questions. Because if everybody did what they really wanted to do, the addictive society assumes that not much work would get done.

Utopian visions aside, simply at the level of the individual, workaholism prevents access to our right work. That fact alone has tremendous societal implications and may explain the progressive numbing of America.

11. Recovery

General Considerations

Before launching into a description of recovery from workaholism, I want to lay out some general considerations—things I believe must be kept in mind throughout our recovery.

Workaholism Is a Disease

If you have made it this far in this book, you will know that I consider work addiction a disease. I am not among those writers who think of it as an interesting aspect of Type A personality, nor a virtue that has to be tempered occasionally.

Work addiction is a disease that has an onset, a progression, and a conclusion. It appears to be both a process addiction (the process of working) and a substance addiction (the adrenaline high). The high is chemical and emotional and the impulse is to get more of it until a progressive numbness sets in. The numbness buffers our ability to monitor our physical and psychological needs and impairs our judgment. Untreated, work addiction ends in death.

In recovery, it is important to remember that we have a disease. We are not bad because we have this disease. In our disease we do harmful things, it is true, but we are separate from the disease.

The Recovery Is a Unique Recovery

For drug and alcohol addicts, abstinence is essential to recovery. For most workaholics, total abstinence is not an option.

Workaholics, like overeaters, must develop a healthy relationship to the work process from the first day of recovery. This problem pertains to the act of working itself. Many aspects of workaholism are amenable to abstinence—rushing, busyness, rescuing, caring, to name a few. But few people can just stop working. To the extent that the job is the site of the fix, workaholics must be very careful to plan a program of recovery that takes into account this constant "temptation." It is for this reason that I believe recovery from work addiction is extremely difficult. It requires support, care, and gentleness, as well as realism about the possible pitfalls.

A System Disease and an Individual Responsibility

I am convinced workaholism is a system disease as well as an individual disease. However, I do not believe that because the system has a disease and individual workaholics are victims of that system that focusing on individuals is "blaming the victims." No matter what happened to us in our dysfunctional families, or in our dysfunctional organizations, the life we now live is our life. It is our responsibility to do our recovery. True, organizations need to do their recovery, too. But until a significant portion of the population is doing their own recovery, we don't have enough clarity to support organizational recovery. I have found that as individuals do their recovery, organizations become healthier. Systems need to recover. Individuals need to recover. If systems are not recovering, that is no excuse for individuals to stay in the disease.

A Wholistic Framework

We have a lot to learn about the recovery from work addiction. I feel fortunate to be writing a book after the founding of Workaholics Anonymous, because this development adds the wisdom of a proven recovery program. Work addiction makes life so out of balance that a holistic approach to recovery is basic.

The recovery should attend to all aspects of the person—physical, emotional, mental, and spiritual. It should be willing to inventory such things as self, family, job, and so on.

I want to say something here about techniques. Just as I am uncomfortable with self-help books that do not address the societal dimension of individual problems, so also am I uneasy with techniques for recovery. I believe that in recovery we need a supportive framework we can follow, and we need to entrust ourselves to such a program precisely because our own efforts have proved futile. However, this is different from taking on techniques that we follow blindly, and that may actually keep us in the addictive process. An example is a woman who said she had no clue when she was overworking that she was alienated from her feelings. She did not experience her emotional alienation, because she used the technique of positive thinking to avoid any depressing feelings. In our recovery, we want to have our real feelings and awarenesses available to us. The positive thinking technique gave the woman a temporary quick fix, but essentially it perpetuated her addiction. This is the problem with techniques and the reason I am wary of them for recovery.

Multiple Options: Danger and Opportunity

The recovering workaholic is faced with many options for healing. It is important to choose those options that feel right for you, but be careful! Part of the disease process of work addiction is flitting from project to project—keeping on the go. The inability to stay with one thing is one aspect of the disease. The tendency to work a thing into the ground is another aspect of the disease. Most people in early recovery learn the wisdom of the slogan "Keep it simple."

Recovering workaholics do have a range of options to choose from, and many of these will be described in more detail later. Among the options are inpatient or outpatient treatment; attendance at Workaholics Anonymous meetings; learning "back-to-life" skills and on-the-job skills; buddy systems; group support; and family programs of recovery.

The Process Is the Goal

In recovery, we have a rude awakening: Everything that made us successful work addicts makes us unsuccessful recovering workaholics. The skills that served us so well in the addiction undermine our recovery. One of the main characteristics of workaholism is that it is a process run wild. It's about rushing, pushing, intensity, and so on. If we attempt the same process with recovery, it will elude us every time. If we set a goal and dash for it like a marathoner, we find ourselves right back in the disease. There simply isn't a quick fix for work addiction.

It is important to remember that many of us began this addiction as children. We've had forty or fifty years of practice. We may as well learn now that we are always going to be recovering, because recovery is learning to live in process. Unlike our control-oriented perfectionistic disease, the process will teach us what we need to learn. We will need to learn to respect it, and in so doing perhaps come to our first real respect of ourselves.

Back-to-Life Skills

Some people have described their workaholism as an experience of being out of their bodies. One woman said she moved around robotlike. The recurrent theme seems to be that workaholics are out of touch with their own lives. The disease is a form of nonliving, as distinct from death, which can be a very lively process! Thus the first challenge for the work addict is to get back to life. This entails doing things that enable us to remember what life is like. We may be so out of touch that we don't know it when we see it or experience it.

Sometimes, in my work as a organizational consultant, I immerse myself in my work with a client for a period of days. Often the work is intense. Several days later, I emerge from the client's building and get in a car to go to the airport. I am immediately aware of the feeling of the air on my skin, the sunlight as distinct from the artificial light of the building, the grass, the sounds, the smells, the news of the world. I know the life I have been living with my client is an artificial environment. It demands my attention and skill, but I do not consider it "real life." I do not look to this environment for my identity. It is temporary. It is interesting. It is not my world.

As work addicts, we need to learn back-to-life skills, because we have come to define our disease as life rather than what it is—nonliving. We believe these tasks, projects, offices, airplanes are the life we must live, when in fact we have choices. We have choices of attitudes, perceptions, and lifestyles. And we have the choice to be separate from what we do. We are not our disease. We will take a look at the following skills:

- abstinence options
- triggers and bottom-line behavior
- daily program for work

Abstinence Options

Abstinence options are options the workaholic has for determining how much contact he or she can have with the disease and still remain sober. Consider at least three abstinence options related to working: stopping work, leaving work, and limiting work. I think each of these options depends on how unmanageable your life has become in relation to the disease.

Stopping work is an option many workaholics choose. For those about to hit the bottom of the workaholic continuum, this choice will already be made for them, because their bodies will burn out. Some stress disease will force them to stop.

Other workaholics take leave from their jobs, ask for a long vacation, or take time off to heal. Many say there is no way to really interrupt the disease process without actually stopping. One woman who took off three months said, "I used the first month to rest and heal physically. In the second month, I took a good look at myself and my priorities. In the third, I edged into some healthy practices for myself. I still felt weary at the end of my break, but I had learned enough about myself and this disease that I wasn't terrified."

Some who stop work go back, but don't do their work workaholically. Others use the break to reorder their priorities, and they never return to that job. A workaholic couple who lived near a ski resort decided to reorder their priorities after both burned out. Both held jet-set jobs with ski companies. They made large sums of money and they paid the price. Physically, they were deteriorating, and their relationship felt shaky. Over a period of three years they downsized their lives. They moved out of their jobs in a trial period, then realized they could not go back to the strain once they saw it for what it was. Then they sold some things they could no longer afford. I met this couple recently, and they are thrilled with their life. They live comfortably, not extravagantly. They do things that have variety and interest. They have a life, not just a job.

Not all of us can afford to stop—at least we think we can't. For some, a variation on leaving work is appropriate abstinence.

Leaving work is certainly an option. Some may choose to leave not the entire job, but an aspect of the job that triggers their disease. A university professor found his work addiction was triggered by expectations to produce articles and books, but he loved teaching. He left his job at one university and joined a college faculty, where teaching was emphasized over publishing. He decided he could leave behind that aspect of his career (and his addictions) to remain in his profession and do what he really wanted to do.

A woman who almost died of stress working in marketing for a large company left the company and became a consultant. She found that consulting gave her the option of deciding how much contact she was willing to have with workaholic organizations. Although she still feels she enters workaholic atmospheres in her client companies, she feels in charge of when and how often, a welcome change from her former environment.

The difference between those who stop and those who leave is that the "stoppers" need a time completely free from the environment that triggers their disease process. The "leavers" may arrange their environment differently, while staying with a job or a career choice.

Limiting work is a third option. These are work addicts who neither stop nor leave. Instead they remain where they are, doing a job, but they put boundaries around their working. The factory worker whose boss locked him out after an eight-hour day is an example. Although the employee did not choose to limit his work, the boss was not willing to encourage workaholism by allowing the man to stay.

Those who limit their work need to understand their own physical and mental limits first. Frankly, I find it difficult to do this without a period of time to "cool out" and evaluate how work addiction is affecting me. Once I know my own limits (a step toward leaving the god illusion), I am then in a better position to make a realistic assessment of what I can and cannot take on.

Many work addicts find it terrifying to set limits. In their self-centeredness, they believe that people have come to count on them for certain things and they are indispensable. Thus it often comes as a shock to discover that things move along without them, usually quite well!

I want to make a distinction between work addiction and work. Work in itself is not the addiction. The addictive process is in the society and the individual. This process gets activated in the individual and results in excessive, compulsive working. Just as alcohol is a substance with certain properties that may or may not be harmful, work may or may not be harmful. The issue is how we use the work. When we use work to prevent ourselves from being in touch with our life process and we need progressively more work, we say we are addicted to work. The addiction then takes on a life of its own. Work is a problem because we use it as a buffer, and consequently do not live our own process.

I use jobs as a key context for workaholism, and indeed jobs are frequently a central issue for many workaholics. However, it is necessary to remember that stopping a job is not necessarily abstinence. One can bring the workaholic process to watching television or tending the garden. Achieving abstinence on the job may not mean recovery, and it is important to deal with the area where our work addiction is killing us first.

After we have dealt with the addiction to work, we still have a range of behavior to contend with. This is why Alcoholics Anonymous makes the very important distinction between dry and sober. We are "dry" when we cease using the substance or process. We are sober when we begin facing our denial, dishonesty, crazy thinking, controlling, perfectionism, isolation, obsessiveness — all those processes described in chapter 3 as characteristic of the disease process. The characteristics are the storm troops of the disease process, and will plague us no matter how much we regulate our actual working, rushing, and busyness.

Triggers and Bottom-Line Behavior

Triggers are behaviors or situations that bring on our workaholism. Identifying the triggers that lead into the disease are often helpful in recovery. For example, a man who is a relationship addict (he uses relationships to stay out of contact with himself and others) found that "hanging out" would lead him into his addiction. He would hang out in cafés hoping to meet someone, or fantasizing about women he saw there—all activities that actually prevented true intimacy. He identified the trigger of hanging out as a bottom-line behavior. By that he meant that he could not engage in hanging out without next moving right into the addiction. If he went that far, he was in trouble immediately.

Food addicts have bottom-line foods. For some sugar is the food that sends them into a binge, so they must assiduously avoid sugar.

A work-addicted man shared that a trigger for him was the leadership position on a team project. He was fine as one of the team. As soon as he was offered the leadership role, however, his sense of inadequacy was hooked and he became compulsive about proving he could do the job. Of course, the harder he tried, the worse it became. He learned that, in his early recovery, a leadership role was deadly for his recovery. Later, as he became stronger, he was able to move into leadership without becoming compulsive.

A housewife workaholic shared that goals were a trigger for her. She had read in a self-help book that every person should set goals and then reach them, and then set more, and so on. She began doing goal setting in every aspect of her life. Then, with no regard for how she was going about achieving her goals, she raced through each day trying to meet her goals. She became a whirling dervish of activity. The goals took on a life of their own; she even dreamed about them. She saw them as an external sign that she was accomplishing something. Internally, she was in chaos. This woman gave up goal setting completely. It is a bottom-line behavior that sends her into her addictive disease.

It is important to identify triggers that set us off into our workaholism. This kind of self-knowledge enables us to see a problem coming and to sidestep it before we are immersed in the addiction. As our recovery progresses, our bottom-line behavior may change. Our bottom line may move "up" to other more subtle behaviors. In early recovery, we may find we are so busy with large troublesome triggers that we are not aware of other aspects of the disease. Later, the smallest dishonesty will trigger us back into our disease—a new bottom line!

Daily Program for Work

Overeaters, debtors, and people who need to maintain a relationship to the addiction from the first day of recovery, find a program helpful. Because their lives are unmanageable around the addiction, the controls need to be turned over to someone or something else. For addicts, this is the powerlessness we feel in the face of the disease and learning to let go is the first step back to sanity. We need to remember that *we* are the ones whose lives are crazy; the purpose of a work program is to reestablish a healthy relationship with a neutral process, work.

Many recovering work addicts develop a daily program with the help of a sponsor (described later). This person can assist in assessing the realism of the plan, help keep it simple and doable. Work plans are tailored to the individual needs of the person, but they usually all contain: (1) number of hours for work, rest, family, play-leisure, alone time; (2) activities at work, with associates, family, volunteer groups, personal health, and so on.

In the early stages of recovery, you may be able to plan only a few hours at a time. Ordinarily, you do the plan for a day at a time. It is important that the plan be a framework to support recovery, not a technique to keep you from taking responsibility for yourself.

It is important to clarify here that time management is not recovery, and it is not what is being described here. Time management can be a helpful adjunct to recovery, just as stress-reduction exercises can help us relax; but we should not fool ourselves that either of these techniques *is* recovery.

In fact, time management can be a problem because it gives the illusion that we can control our disease. This puts us right back into the disease, since control is one of its characteristics.

Another approach to this plan is suggested by Debtors Anonymous, the group for people whose lives are unmanageable around money. Debtors and money addicts meet with two people who have sobriety around their money issues. The debtor lists all his or her financial assets and all debts. After discussing the present situation—which, by the time of this meeting, feels critical for the debtor—he or she develops a spending plan. The purpose of the meeting, called a "pressure group," is to take the pressure off the debtor who is attempting to handle the disease process in isolation and to put pressure on him or her to develop a plan that will stop the downward financial spiral. The two supporters are there to keep the debtor from agreeing to things he or she cannot realistically accomplish, like paying off all credit card bills but not budgeting for food for a month. The debtor keeps checking in with these sponsors. In addition, most debtors keep a daily record of every penny they spend. In their disease, they are often unconscious about money. It comes and goes and they have no idea where or how it is spent. The daily log of expenses is a crucial tool for sobriety.

Work addicts use a similar program to aid their recovery. By meeting with people who have sobriety around work, we come out of our isolation. We list in precise detail a typical day or days. I think it is important to describe any physical and emotional symptoms we are feeling, as they are a big part of the disease. This process aids us in confronting our denial about the extent of our workaholism. I was part of such a process with a woman workaholic. After it was over, she said to me that as she described a day and her physical symptoms, she saw shock on my face. (I was very concerned, as she was showing extreme stress.) "Seeing the shock on your face, I suddenly realized how sick I was making myself. I let myself feel how much trouble I was in with this addiction."

Listing our activities in precise detail is important, because work addicts tend to hide their stash. We may have little activities stored away we don't show. The two support people can probe, "Are you sure that's all you do between lunch and 1 P.M.?" They help jog our memories and keep us honest.

After compiling our day's list, we go over it with the support people, identifying those activities and hours that are killing us, contributing to our obsessiveness, or are humanly impossible. Again, doing this with people who have a healthy relationship with work is good, for they add perspective and can point out crazy thinking. In our compulsion to get well, we do health workaholically!

A woman who worked mornings and had a neighborhood day-care center in the afternoon was enthusiastically going to "rush" from her work plan meeting to close down her day-care center that day. The support people asked her to consider slowing down, checking out the steps she'd need to take to close the center in a responsible manner, and go about it over a period of several months. This was a useful suggestion, for she frequently raced into projects without thinking through the consequences. As a result, she got in over her head. The support people were asking her to change her process, since the process of her disease was the thing that was killing her, not the fact that she had a day-care center.

The woman took the advice of her supporters and, as she began the process of closing the center, she discovered that a slower pace resulted in more energy. Also, her employees were less frantic because they were not responding to her erratic directives. Before long it became evident that the day-care enterprise was not the problem. It did not require elimination. *How* she ran her business was the problem. As she worked her daily work plan, she became healthier, a better employer, and a fine manager.

The wonderful thing about recovery from work addiction is that the outcomes are always surprises. This is probably not good news for those of us who like control! By being willing to put her recovery first and, if necessary, close her business, the woman became open to her process. We have to be willing to give up everything in order to recover—if we don't recover, we usually lose everything anyway. Often, when we let go, we find out that we don't have to give up the things we thought we would lose.

None of us has the courage to do the action that may be required of us months from now. The beauty of a day-by-day work plan is that it puts our recovery in manageable, one-step-at-a-time sequences.

In summary, three back-to-life processes support our early recovery:

1. Identify options for abstinence: stopping, leaving, or limiting work.
2. Be explicit about the things that trigger us into our work addiction. Decide the bottom-line behavior.
3. Develop a daily program for work that includes all aspects of life. If possible, meet with two people whose relationship to work is healthy, and do a thorough inventory of a day or week. From that meeting develop the work plan. Do it day by day.

On-the-Job Skills

Work addiction affects all aspects of our lives, and many work addicts practice their addiction primarily on the job. Their focus becomes the job and the other areas of life are left behind.

Work Inventory and Plan of Action

The same process for planning described above can be utilized on the job. Sue August, an organizational consultant,

combines a plan of action with a support group to give maximum resources to workaholic employees. She finds that work
addicts are most dishonest about their projects. These are the
hidden stash of the addict at work. In doing their inventory,
she insists workaholics come clean about how many projects
they are doing and what they have waiting "in the wings."

Support Groups

Support groups are invaluable for the recovering workaholic
in the organization. In several organizations, the productivity
consultant had unearthed the fact that uneven productivity
was caused by the workaholic pattern of several employees.
He met with each person individually and then brought them
together in a group. A few were binge workers, so their productivity was erratic. One was a work anorexic, and production was at the last minute. The rest were relentless workers.
By sharing their stories, they were able to see some common
threads in their processes. Each person made a work plan and
chose a buddy from the group to share the plan with. The
group has made a commitment to meet weekly for one hour
for support. In addition, each person calls his or her buddy
and reviews the work plan for that day.

This process builds in support, takes the workaholic out
of isolation, and also has accountability. There is no blame
built into this process. The idea is to learn about the disease
of workaholism through one another's stories and to give support for healing in concrete ways.

I think a plan of work and support for recovery at work
are essential for recovery. Many workaholics feel ashamed
about their workaholism; and, to the extent that their lives are
becoming more chaotic, they begin to hide their activities
from those who might observe them. The groups described
above created a safe place for work-addicted employees. A
safe place is a group in which there is no judgment. You are

not considered a bad person because you are in the group. Only in such groups is honesty possible — and the more honest work addicts are, the greater their chance for recovery.

Role of the Organization

Organizations can support employees in recovery from work addiction, as well as face the addictive process in the organization as a whole. The tools they can use include

- education
- intervention
- changing the corporate culture
- cost-effectiveness

Education

Companies must educate employees about the characteristics of workaholism. Such education can easily be incorporated into existing programs on stress. However, it is essential to remember that the temporarily stressed-out worker is not the same as a workaholic. Workers need to recognize the difference between periodic stress and a potentially fatal disease. Companies can encourage treatment for workaholism by identifying it as an addictive disease worthy of attention by EAPs and human resource departments.

Interventions

Companies should plan and carry out interventions with active workaholics. As work addicts sink further into their disease, they tend to develop elaborate cons, which deceive themselves and supervisors. Intervention is necessary to interrupt this pattern and stop the self-destructive behavior. It is helpful for workaholics when others give feedback about behavior they are observing in the work addict.

An intervention is a meeting in which concerned people meet face-to-face with the work addict. In a nonjudgmental way, each person describes the behavior of the addict, states his or her concern and how the addict's behavior is affecting them. The meeting concludes with each person sharing with the addict the consequences for the addict if he or she does not seek treatment or begin recovery. EAP and addiction counselors can train groups in successful intervention with workaholic employees. (Intervention techniques are described more fully in the next section.)

Changing the Corporate Culture

Corporations must take a hard look at their cultures and systems. Just as individuals can be workaholic, the organization can practice the same disease. CEOs and managers would do well to ask themselves if they are contributing to workaholism by unrealistic expectations, impossible job descriptions, and a corporate culture that pursues profit above everything else.

The current fascination with excellent companies leads me to wonder if these aspirations are really healthy in the long run. For example, Tom Peters and Nancy Austin say that the cost of excellence is the giving up of

> family vacations, little league games, birthday dinners, evenings, weekends and lunch hours, gardening, reading, movies and most other pastimes. We have a number of friends whose marriages or partnerships crumbled under the weight of their devotion to a dream . . . We are frequently asked if it is possible to "have it all"—a full satisfying personal life and a full satisfying hard working professional one. Our answer is "no."[1]

The pursuit of excellence is highly touted in corporations today. I consider the above description a prescription for workaholism.

Cost-Effectiveness

Companies need to ask themselves if it is cost-effective to continue down the workaholic path. My research shows that it is an illusion to believe that work addicts benefit companies. Quite the contrary is true. Organizations are spending money rectifying workaholic employees mistakes. They are paying increased health care costs for stressed-out employees. They are seeing creativity and productivity drop as late-stage workaholics suffer from forgetfulness and one-dimensional thinking. They are having difficulty attracting gifted workers, because the corporate atmosphere is polluted by a workaholic ethic and consciously healthy people avoid such settings. Not to see this is to participate in the denial system of the addict. Conversely, companies that address the problem of a workaholic culture and the individual workaholic stand to benefit. Companies will salvage talented and dedicated workers. Companies also may find their productivity and creativity on the rise, proving once again that individual and organizational health are the ultimate rewards. They are also inextricably linked.

When You Are the Workaholic's Loved One

As hard as we try to hide our addictions, they are not private. Our isolating and secrets keep us in the addictive process. Often, as addicts get crazier, so also do their families. Families and loved ones have responsibility for their health even when living with a workaholic—especially when living with one. Loved ones can take concrete steps.

Take Care of Yourself

Families and loved ones must take care of themselves first. This sounds like the last thing you would do, since your concern is for the workaholic. But part of the disease process of workaholism is to get the family hooked into the disease, thereby protecting the work addict's supply. The best thing you can do for the workaholic in your life is to take care of yourself.

To take care of yourself means unhooking from the workaholic's rushing, busyness, franticness. It means admitting you are powerless over the work addict's disease. You may have spent many years focused on the workaholic and be bound to that person by ties of resentment and hurt. Many loved ones of workaholics don't know what they need for themselves, because they have spent so many years externally referenced on the workaholic.

A woman married to a workaholic had resented her husband for years because he would not go on vacation. Because she would not take a vacation without him, she felt deprived and angry. As she unhooked from his disease, she began to deal with her own needs and decided a vacation was her responsibility. Now she takes vacations alone or with friends all the time. Taking responsibility for yourself does mean that the old patterns of relationships will change. If you are firmly entrenched in the notion that couples must travel together, then you will stay stuck in the misery of letting your life be controlled by the workaholic's broken promises.

The jet-set couple who chose to downsize their economic needs did their recovery together. This is not always the case. The man confided to me that even if his wife had decided to remain with her job, he was clear that no real life was possible for him given his workaholism. "I was willing to do anything I needed to do to get well, even if it meant renegotiating my relationship with my wife. It could have meant a split between us. I was too sick to be much of a mate anyway."

Remember, as a loved one of a workaholic, you get immersed in your own addictive process in response to life with the addict. So taking responsibility for your recovery is just as important as the workaholic getting well. You should seek support through groups like Al-Anon, Codependents Anonymous, and Adult Children of Alcoholics groups. All of these groups are able to support and teach us about ourselves and our part in the addictive process.

Intervention

Plan and carry out an intervention with the workaholic. An intervention is a structured meeting between the workaholic and concerned family and friends. Its purpose is to intervene on the disease process. The intervention process was developed by the Johnson Institute in Minnesota in the 1950s. It was designed to "raise the bottom" for the addicts. The conventional wisdom had been that an addict will not get help until he or she hits bottom. For many people, bottom meant losing everything—home, job, social standing, physical health. The Johnson Institute asked, "Does a person have to go all the way to bottom and lose everything? Is it possible to intervene earlier?" The intervention process was their answer.

This process puts pressure on the addict. The loved ones give the workaholic notice that they will no longer support the disease process. They love the workaholic, but they hate the disease, and there are consequences for the work addict choosing to stay in it.

I recommend that you be trained in this process by qualified addictions counselors before trying it. Interventions have distinct steps. In step one, prior to the actual meeting with the workaholic, each person attending the intervention needs to answer the following questions: How has the workaholic's disease affected me? What do I need to do to take responsibility for myself and take care of myself? You should not rush through these questions. Chances are you've spent years around the work addict, and you may have numbed yourself to the point where you don't know what you need at first.

To prepare for the actual intervention, the group meets and each person develops a nonjudgmental description of the behaviors seen in the workaholic, the concerns felt, the effect the behaviors have on him or her, and the consequences the person is willing to carry out if the work addict does not seek help. Two key terms to remember are *nonjudgmental* and *consequences.* Nonjudgmental means that the group is not gathered to heap blame. Workaholics have a disease; they are not their disease. Consequences means that you should never promise a consequence you are not fully prepared to carry out. Don't dramatically threaten to divorce a workaholic spouse unless you have thought through that process and intend to do it.

In the case of a workaholic factory employee who insisted upon working twelve hours a day, the plant supervisor did a one-man intervention when he took the man's keys and locked him out of the plant. Earlier the supervisor had said, "I see you working overtime every day. The line is slowing down [nonjudgmental description]. I am concerned for your health and possible accidents on line to you or others [effect on him, concern]. I want you to leave at five o'clock every day. If you don't, I'm taking away your plant keys [consequences]."

Interventions can be effective because they turn up the heat under the workaholic. They get the workaholic's attention. However, they are no panacea. Sometimes they work, sometimes they do not. It is important for the family and friends to remember that the workaholic will have to choose recovery. No one can do that for the addict. And the loved ones, having done all they can, need to go forward with their own healing. Nothing more is asked of them.

When the Organization Is the Workaholic

Every week my office receives letters from people in organizations who are recovering from work addiction. The letters carry one of two themes. One theme goes: I got healthy, my family is getting healthy, but my workplace is workaholic. I go to work and I feel crazy. I am considering leaving. The other theme goes: I got healthy and I got fired. Conclusion: Workaholic organizations are losing or getting rid of some of their healthiest people.

When the organization is the workaholic, you have a range of options. Some people do leave. They join other companies, although that is a risk, for workaholic organizations abound. Some people start their own businesses or go into partnership with others. Some move to a part of the organization that is less affected by workaholism. I knew a man who preferred making lateral moves in his organization rather than hopping on the vertical management track. The money was a little less and the stress was considerably less. Still others take early retirement and use the time to explore new possibilities. In the workaholic organization, the issue is to take care of yourself and see what you need. When you find yourself surviving the company's workaholism by becoming workaholic yourself, you are in trouble.

I know organizations that have developed informal networks of support open to all employees and used widely by the recovering addicts in the organization. One organization, a gigantic worldwide software manufacturer, has a computerized "serenity network" that every employee can access. All over the world, people in recovery can send a message over the network. Each day a small meditation for the day appears on the screen. Individuals who are struggling with some aspect of their addiction may go on-line. Messages of support come from the United States, Europe, and Southeast Asia within minutes. Another organization has a support group for workaholics that meets weekly for an hour over lunch. (Of course! Workaholics do two things at once whenever possible!)

Although these efforts appear small, I believe they are

more widespread than we imagine. They give hope for improving our lives at work and perhaps improving organizations themselves.

When Your Life Is Coming Apart

When your life is coming apart due to advanced workaholism, you probably won't be reading this book! Since you *are* reading this book, however, you are probably in the later stages of the disease.

You are experiencing blackouts, headaches, high blood pressure, ulcers. You are having difficulty sleeping. Your relationships are on hold. Emotionally, you feel dead. You are moody, unpredictable. People give you a wide berth. You feel you haven't time to see a doctor. You are working constantly or in intense spurts. You are hiding work or you are paralyzed by inactivity. Inside you hurt. Mentally, you hear yourself saying, "I can't keep going like this." You are scared. You are in trouble.

When you are at this stage of the disease you need drastic action, because your life is literally in danger. You are working yourself to death. I recommend two things at this point.

One: Stop.

Two: Seek treatment immediately. If you have any shred of sensibility left, you will stop. Your body and mind are on overdrive. If you do not stop yourself, your body will do it for you and you risk long-term consequences.

You may be able to stop temporarily, but until you actually treat the underlying disease process of the workaholic, your disease is just pausing, gathering steam to carry on. Consider treatment at an inpatient addictions treatment center. Workaholism is only recently being recognized as an addiction, so you are not likely to find a center specializing in treatment of this specific addiction. However, many treatment centers treat codependency and recognize the link between codependency and work addiction. Addiction centers have both inpatient and outpatient programs. Do the treatment that fits for you. Remember that it is not just a matter of stress management. You can take a workshop on that at your local YMCA with dubious results, I believe. You need a setting that facilitates your healing and understands the addictive disease process. You create your life, and you will need to start taking responsibility for it. It is important to begin now, before it is too late.

Workaholics Anonymous Twelve-Step Programs

Marilyn Machlowitz, one of the first researchers to write a serious book about workaholism, decided that workaholics could not be "cured" completely, that it was in their blood. She subsequently observed that there was no Workaholics Anonymous, nor should there be. Five years after she uttered those words, the first Workaholics Anonymous groups were springing up around the country. They were successfully applying the principles of recovery developed fifty years earlier by Alcoholics Anonymous—the acknowledged leader in the treatment of alcoholism.

I recommend Workaholics Anonymous as the most effective process for treating work addiction. I believe that all the other techniques you read about—nutrition, exercise, visualizing, scheduling—are fine, but not as the core of a recovery program. Thirty minutes on the rowing machine may help reduce your blood pressure, a symptom; it will not address the addictive disease process.

To face into the addictive disease process you need to experience that you are powerless over your work addiction and that everything you've tried has failed. It is time to turn your life over to a power greater than yourself.

Workaholics Anonymous is based on the Twelve Steps (reproduced in the Appendix). It also offers some specific tools of recovery.[2] These tools include

- sponsors
- meetings
- telephone contact
- work plan
- service

Sponsors

Sponsors are recovering work addicts who guide you through a program of recovery. Your sponsor may assist you with the work plan or may lead you through the Twelve Steps. Sponsors help workaholics avoid isolation. Also, they are usually people who have a longer recovery or sobriety than you have. They can speak from experience and lend hope that recovery is possible.

Meetings

Workaholics Anonymous meetings take place whenever two or more work addicts gather. The tradition of Twelve-Step meetings is to share experiences through stories, and to share strength and hope. Meetings are invaluable because they reduce the isolation and give us the opportunity to identify our behaviors in our stories and in others. We learn the common characteristics of the disease in meetings. Also, meetings are anonymous; you don't have to worry about your personal or professional reputation. Furthermore, you can speak freely in meetings as everything said there remains there.

Telephone Contact

The telephone doesn't have to be a medium of the disease. It can aid in recovery too! Recovering workaholics use phone contact as a way of staying linked between meetings. This means you can call for support when you are feeling particularly compulsive. Using the telephone this way is a form of asking for help.

Work Plan

As described earlier, the work plan is a concrete way of committing to a new style of life. By having it in writing, and not just in your head, you've made a visible sign of your intention to carry it out. You can also use writing to clarify feelings and to get in touch with those aspects of the disease that drive you into relentless working.

Service

Twelve-Step programs the world over counteract the self-centeredness of the disease by service to other addicts. This is basic to recovery and is part of the basic purpose of any self-help movement. The service can be sharing the message of your recovery with other workaholics or it can be putting away chairs at meetings or any number of other activities.

These are the basic tools of recovery of Workaholics Anonymous. They are time tested. They are the tools used by millions of recovering addicts the world over. If used conscientiously, they carry a powerful promise that has come true for scores of recovering people. The promise is this: "Rarely has a person failed who has thoroughly followed this path with rigorous honesty." I know of no other program for work addicts that dares to make such a promise nor that makes good on such a promise as often as the Twelve-Step groups do.

On the work addiction continuum, the bottom is death, and before that is spiritual bankruptcy. Twelve-Step groups are openly spiritual, not religious. They are not a religion. Their wisdom is that they recognize that work addiction is a disease of the soul. It affects us in the deepest part of our being. I think we become soul sick. The spiritual dimension of Workaholics Anonymous is a welcome addition. Since the churches themselves are dysfunctional with workaholism, it is good to have a place to go where dogma and petty arguments have no place and where faith in a Higher Power is the priority. This recovery brings us full circle. We regain our bodies, which are racked with stress. We see our relationships for what they really are. We have access to our true work. Ultimately, we get back ourselves and our lives more abundantly.

Just as work addiction has an identifiable progression ending in death, so recovery has a progressive result in living. The following scale shows some of the major points along that path.

THE WORK ADDICTION SCALE

Progression of Recovery →

- Joyfully alive, living a day at a time
- Intimacy with self, others, work
- Secondary addictions confronted
- Boundaries set appropriately
- Compulsiveness diminishes in all areas
- All decisions made with awareness of priority of recovery
- Ability to distinguish between being into workaholism and when not
- Reawakening of feelings
- Sense of humility; realistic about abilities
- Family obligations met
- Relationships reestablished
- Sleeps regularly; food and exercise integrated in healthy manner
- Gradual recovery of physical health
- Limits hours at work; takes time off
- Spirituality returns
- Develops work plan; uses tools of recovery program
- Feels optimistic about possibilities
- Feels grief at loss of addiction
- Begins attendance at Twelve-Step program
- Seeks treatment
- Open to support; input of others
- Actively seeks help
- Admits having a disease
- Understanding disease concept of workaholism
- Admission of powerlessness

The Progression of the Disease →

Early Stage

- Rushing, busyness, caring, rescuing
- Inability to say "No"
- Constantly thinking of work
- Compulsive list making
- Exaggerated belief in one's own abilities
- No days off
- Hours exceed 40 consistently

Middle Stage

- Increase in other addictions begins: Food, alcohol, relationship, money, etc.
- Social life diminished or nonexistent
- Begin giving up relationships and relationship obligations
- Attempts to change fail
- Physically worn out, difficulty sleeping
- Periods of comatose staring into space
- Blackouts at work, on the road

Late Stage

- Chronic headaches, backaches, high blood pressure, ulcers, depression
- Stroke, serious illness, hospitalization
- Emotional deadness
- Moral and spiritual bankruptcy
- Death

Epilogue:
Coming Back to Life

What are the implications for ourselves, our families, our organizations and the society if we do not address work addiction? We have seen the effects of this disease at all levels. Across the board, it means dulling of our sensibilities, fascination with short-term results to the detriment of the long-term solution, alienation from our essential selves, ethical deterioration, and death.

Is there not irony in the fact that the symbol of the typical modern U.S. man or woman in the rest of the world is the workaholic? This is a potent symbol. No wonder such silence resounds around work addiction. To tamper with it is to tamper with something very close to the American heart—its addictive process in its finest form.

I believe that the 1990s is a time for a radical reordering of social and personal priorities. Already the environmental crisis alone has demonstrated the need for a global shift in values. If we love the universe and wish to live here in the future, we must pursue policies out of a new paradigm. But what does this have to do with the individual workaholic? Everything, I would submit.

Our society is based on the old notion of Newtonian physics, which sees humans as machines and the society the same. In this view, you can beat it up, use it up, and discard it. Individuals are largely victims of the society and, lacking resources to solve their own problems, are exempt from

responsibility. Much of our social policy is based on the prem-
ise that things are so bad, people can't help themselves. We've
become objects even to ourselves, and we do not participate
intimately in our lives.

A society that operates out of these antiquated principles
has many casualties. Often the first to fall are those who are
most invested in the system. Workaholics are walking examples of the dysfunction of our society. They are reminders and
symbols that our social vision of the good life went awry. The
reason I'm concerned about the silence surrounding workaholism, is that it points to a deep-seated denial that is socially
destructive. We cannot live with the schizophrenia of saving
the earth while killing ourselves. This is my concern, and it is
why I cannot treat work addiction as solely an individual
problem.

But still, I have reason for hope. Recovery from work
addiction and any addiction is a paradigm shift of unprecedented significance. Recovering people do not put blame "out
there." Regardless of how terrible our lives, how many
chances missed, we are finally, ultimately, responsible for
ourselves. And so we begin, day by day, step by step, the slow
process of coming back to life.

How many out there are doing this active recovery from
workaholism I can only guess. Surely their numbers are not
legion, yet I know they are growing. They are part of an evolv-
ing consciousness that sees new human possibilities. They
are the forerunners of a new work ethic. These are the ones
who no longer live to work. They work to live and find it life
giving. In the end, their lives are reclaimed and so, at last, is
work.

Appendix

The Twelve Steps of Workaholics Anonymous

1. We admitted we were powerless over our compulsive working—that our lives had become unmanageable.
2. Came to believe that a Power greater than ourselves could restore us to sanity.
3. Made a decision to turn our will and our lives over to the care of God *as we understood Him.*
4. Made a searching and fearless moral inventory of ourselves.
5. Admitted to God, to ourselves, and to another human being the exact nature of our wrongs.
6. Were entirely ready to have God remove all these defects of character.
7. Humbly asked Him to remove our shortcomings.
8. Made a list of all persons we had harmed, and became willing to make amends to them all.
9. Made direct amends to such people wherever possible, except when to do so would injure them or others.
10. Continued to take personal inventory, and when we were wrong promptly admitted it.
11. Sought through prayer and meditation to improve our conscious contact with God *as we understood Him*, praying only for the knowledge of His will for us and the power to carry that out.
12. Having had a spiritual awakening as the result of these steps, we tried to carry this message to workaholics and to practice these principles in all our affairs.

The Twelve Steps of Alcoholics Anonymous

1. We admitted we were powerless over alcohol—that our lives had become unmanageable.
2. Came to believe that a Power greater than ourselves could restore us to sanity.
3. Made a decision to turn our will and our lives over to the care of God *as we understood Him.*
4. Made a searching and fearless moral inventory of ourselves.
5. Admitted to God, to ourselves, and to another human being the exact nature of our wrongs.
6. Were entirely ready to have God remove all these defects of character.
7. Humbly asked Him to remove our shortcomings.
8. Made a list of all persons we had harmed, and became willing to make amends to them all.
9. Made direct amends to such people wherever possible, except when to do so would injure them or others.
10. Continued to take personal inventory, and when we were wrong promptly admitted it.
11. Sought through prayer and meditation to improve our conscious contact with God *as we understood Him,* praying only for the knowledge of His will for us and the power to carry that out.
12. Having had a spiritual awakening as the result of these steps, we tried to carry this message to alcoholics and to practice these principles in all our affairs.

Notes

Preface: A Resounding Silence

1. Bryan E. Robinson, Ph.D., *Work Addiction: Hidden Legacies of Adult Children* (Deerfield Beach, FL: Health Communications, 1989).

Introduction: A Killer Disease

1. John O. Neikirk. "Workaholism: The Pain Others Applaud," *Focus Magazine* (August/September 1988): 1.
2. Bryan E. Robinson, Ph.D., *Work Addiction: Hidden Legacies of Adult Children* (Deerfield Beach, FL: Health Communications, 1989), 24.

1. Workaholism: Reality and Myths

1. Winifred Gallagher, "Success," *American Health* (April 1989): 55.

2. Four Types of Work Addicts

1. Harold Johnson, quoted in Anne Wilson Schaef, *Laugh I Thought I'd Die... If I Didn't* (New York: Ballantine: 1990).

3. Characteristics of Workaholics

1. Walter Kiechel, III, "The Workaholic Generation," *Fortune* (April 10, 1989): 51.
2. Ronald Yates, "Japanese live... and die... for their work," *Chicago Tribune* (November 13, 1988): 1.
3. Joel F. Lehrer, MD and Leila M. Hover, MLS, "Fatigue Syndrome," *Journal of the American Medical Association*, Vol. 259, No. 6: 842–43.

5. Women & Workaholism

1. Anne Wilson Schaef, *Women's Reality* (San Francisco: Harper & Row, 1981).
2. Colette Dowling, *Perfect Women* (New York: Summit Books, 1988), 16.
3. Ellen Sue Stern, *The Indispensable Woman* (New York: Bantam, 1988), 15.

6. Men & Workaholism

1. Anne Wilson Schaef, *Women's Reality* (San Francisco: Harper & Row, 1981).

7. The Family & Workaholism

1. Nancy Gibbs, "How America Has Run Out of Time," *Time* (April 24, 1989): 61.

9. The Workaholic Organization

1. See Anne Wilson Schaef and Diane Fassel, *The Addictive Organization* (San Francisco, Harper & Row, 1988). In this book we describe the organization as addictive in four ways: (1) active addicts in organizations destroy organizational effectiveness; (2) codependents replicate their dysfunctional behavior in organizations; (3) the organization is the addictive substance in the lives of workers; (4) the organizations are addicts in their structures and processes.
2. Tim Lucas, "Business Faces Newest Crisis," *The Indianapolis Star* (June 6, 1988).

10. Why Are We Doing This to Ourselves?

1. All of Schaef's books since 1986 develop some aspect of this theme. The key work, *When Society Becomes An Addict* (San Francisco: Harper & Row, 1986), lays out the basic framework of this idea and is indispensable for understanding the concept of an underlying addictive process. Schaef's other works are highly recommended as well.

2. Harlan Ellison, 1989 Spring Conference of Western States Advertising Agencies Association in Rancho Mirage, California; quoted in the trade publication *Advertising Age* (Spring, 1989), 12.

3. Schaef, *When Society Becomes An Addict.*

4. A. Lawrence Chickering, "Denial Hardens The Drug Crisis," *Wall Street Journal* (July 25, 1988).

5. *Ibid.*

6. Dave Todd, "A Nation in Denial: Chaos and the Politics of Dysfunction" (July 1989): 7 (Paper circulated privately).

7. *Ibid.*

8. Stephen Nogg and Lorraine Davis, "Burnout: A Comparative Analysis of Personality and Environmental Variables," *Psychological Reports*, Vol. 57, (#3, part 2) 1985: 1319–26.

9. Thomas Merton, *The Sign of Jonas* (New York: Harcourt, Brace and Company, 1953), 251.

10. Kurt Vonnegut, "Weapons Junkies," *Fellowship* (September 1987): 10.

11. William Beecher, "Battle Over Tower Nomination May Leave Some Lasting Scars," *Star Tribune* (March 10, 1989): 14.

11. Recovery

1. Tom Peters and Nancy Austin, *A Passion for Excellence* (New York: Warner, 1985), 495–96.

2. For more information on Workaholics Anonymous, if you live on the East Coast, write Workaholics Anonymous, Westchester Community College, Westchester Self-Help Clearinghouse, Academic Arts Building, Valhalla, NY 10595. If you are on the West Coast, write Workaholics Anonymous, 511 Sir Francis Drake C-170, Greenbrae, CA 94904

Index